THE AWAKENING OF INDIA

THE AWAKENING OF INDIA

FORTY YEARS AMONG THE TELUGUS

WILLIAM ARTHUR STANTON

GYAN

Published by

Gyan Publishing House
5, Ansari Road
Daryaganj, New Delhi-110002
Phone: 011-47034999, 9811692060
E-mail: books@gyanbooks.com

Distribution Network
gyanbooks.com
India, USA, Canada, UK, Australia

ISBN: 978-93-7169-663-0 (PB)

First Published, 1950

2nd Impression 2025

Printed at: Gyan Press, Delhi.

THE AWAKENING OF INDIA
Author: WILLIAM ARTHUR STANTON

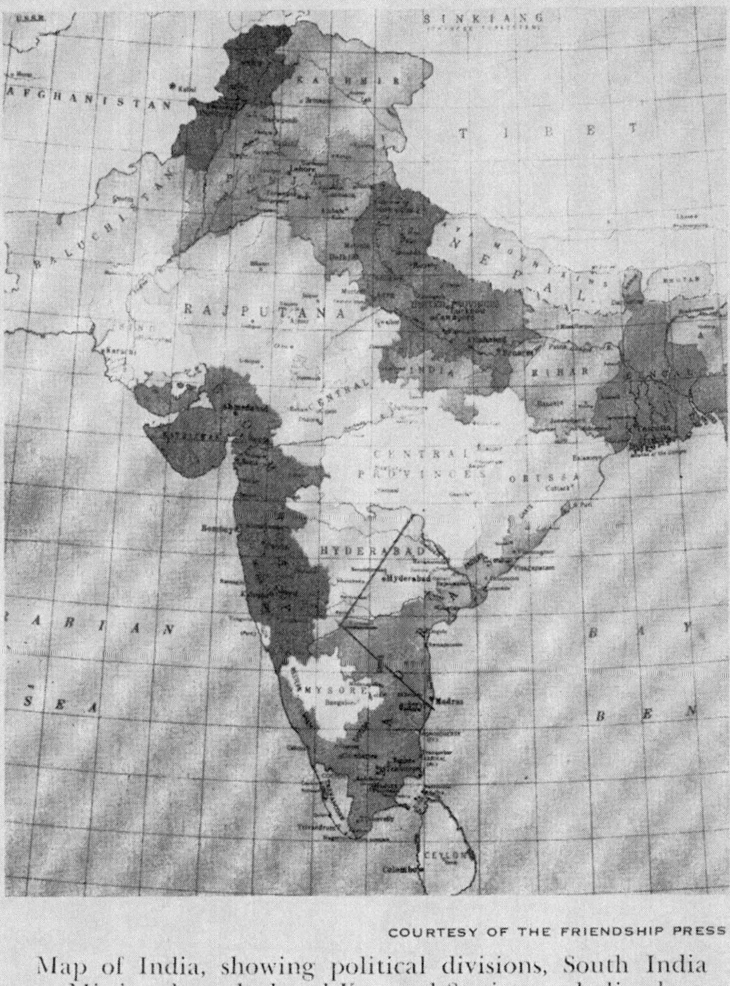

COURTESY OF THE FRIENDSHIP PRESS

Map of India, showing political divisions, South India Mission demarked and Kurnool Station underlined.

The Awakening of India

Forty Years Among the Telugus

by

WILLIAM ARTHUR STANTON

TO

BETTY, ED, AND KATHY

WHOSE BRIGHT, SWEET FACES

AND LOVING LAUGHTER MADE OUR INDIAN

HOME A DELIGHT

Is there some desert or some pathless sea
Where thou, good God of angels, wilt send me?
Some oak for me to rend; some sod,
Some rock for me to break;
Some handful of his corn to take
And scatter far afield,
Till it, in turn, shall yield
Its hundredfold
Of grains of gold
To feed the waiting children of my God?
Show me the desert, Father, or the sea.
Is it thine enterprise? Great God, send me.
And though this body lie where ocean rolls
Count me among all faithful souls.

—Edward Everett Hale

PREFACE

This book covers the years my wife and I spent as missionaries of the American Baptist Foreign Mission Society in the old "Lone Star Mission", South India, at Kurnool, our mission station. It is the story of the Gospel in India—story of a dynamic power, working in that ancient land, transforming lives, uprooting old customs, sweeping away old landmarks, making all things new. It is the story of a great spiritual awakening among the untouchables of India—the story of open doors, of white harvest fields, of struggle and triumph, of darkness and light; the story of vast movements—political, social and religious, sweeping over awakened India for a quarter of a century. In many forms the story runs, but the theme is one—*God at work in the hearts of men!*

The book is timely. India is on the front page today—the heart of Asia. The story of India's struggle for freedom—the awakening of a great people from the long sleep of centuries, is soul-stirring and deeply moving. A whole chapter is given to Mahatma Gandhi, crusader and saint, prophet of non-violence, arousing his people, not by the sword, but by the power of "soul-force", to a mighty struggle for freedom.

In the midst of these stirring and momentous movements, quietly and undismayed, we have lived and worked, often discouraged, but never cast down, assured that He who called us that night in the old academy chapel at Hamilton, New York was sufficient for all these things. Touring the villages, preaching the good news of the Kingdom, teaching the lowly and the outcaste the things of God, planting the Christian church in the soil of India, developing self-support and self-government, ministering to the poor and needy, training

Indian workers for Christian leadership—this was our work in those early days and on this foundation we built, persistantly and without interruption, through forty years of fruitful service.

In sending out this little book, we would not fail to express our deep sense of obligation and gratitude to Dr. Randolph L. Howard, formerly Foreign Secretary of the American Baptist Foreign Mission Society; Dr. Jesse R. Wilson, Home Secretary; Dr. Paul Conrad, Secretary of Stewardship of the Northern Baptist Convention; Miss Dorothy A. Stevens, Director of Missionary Education, Northern Baptist Convention, and Dr. Joseph C. Robbins, formerly Foreign Secretary of the American Baptist Foreign Mission Society for twenty-five years and ex-President of the Northern Baptist Convention—all of whom very kindly read the manuscript and offered most helpful advice and encouragement.

WILLIAM ARTHUR STANTON

Montclair,
May 30, 1949.

TABLE OF CONTENTS

LIST OF ILLUSTRATIONS

THE AWAKENING OF INDIA

I

INDIA'S STRUGGLE FOR FREEDOM

WHEN Fanny and I arrived in Bombay on September 30, 1921, after furlough in the homeland, we found ourselves in the midst of the Non-co-operation movement of which Gandhi was the acknowledged leader. Gandhi caps were everywhere in evidence. Congress "volunteers" were picketing the shops and mills. Processions, *hartals* (boycotts) and demonstrations were the order of the day. Business was at a standstill. Revolution was in the air. The Non-co-operation movement had gained a tremendous hold on large sections of the people. In some of the disturbed areas every schoolboy was shouting "*Gandhi-ki-jai,*" (Victory to Gandhi"). The aim of the movement was no other than the overthrow of the existing government and the establishment of *swaraj,* (independence). It sought to accomplish this end through passive resistance or non-violence, aiming gradually to bring the machinery of the government to a standstill and force it to abdicate. Though professedly non-violent in character, by its disregard of the laws of the land, its organization of "volunteers" for picketing, boycott and intimidation and its unceasing propaganda against the government, it aroused the passions of the people and gathered to itself the forces of lawlessness to such a degree that, unless suppressed, it could end only in bloodshed and revolution.

The year 1922 opened in turmoil. Everywhere Congress forces were openly arrayed against the government. The campaign of non-co-operation was in full swing. The cry of the Gandhiites, "*Paralyze the government*" was everywhere heard. Village officers were resigning their posts and joining the non-co-operation. *Ryots* (farmers) were refusing to pay taxes, openly defying the government. Non-co-operation was rapidly developing into violent revolution; the forces of lawlessness and anarchy set in motion by the preaching of Gandhi and his followers were steadily gaining strength and getting out of hand. In February occurred the tragedy of Chauri-Chaura in the northwest provinces, in which a frenzied mob of three thousand people attacked the police station and set it on fire, burning alive the devoted men within its walls. Never since the days of the Mutiny had the country faced so serious a crisis.

At last the government, so long forbearing and seemingly irresolute, took action. On March 10, 1922, Gandhi was arrested at Ahmadabad and, after a swift trial, was sentenced to six years' imprisonment. This decisive action, striking at the root of the agitation, immediately restored confidence in the government and was the turning point in the situation. From this time on the government adopted a strong and vigorous policy of law enforcement. *Ryots* who refused to pay taxes were summarily dealt with and their cattle seized. Agitators preaching sedition were locked up in jail. Riot and disorder were suppressed with a strong hand. By the month of May the situation was well in hand and order restored.

But the Non-co-operation movement, though suppressed for the moment, was only driven underground. Again it would rise, and with renewed strength and power. Gandhi, the great leader, though cast into prison was not conquered. The struggle was on; India would yet be free. A million voices were crying, *"Gandhi-ki-jai!"*

India Awakening

Now what is the meaning of this struggle, this uprising of

a great people? India is in a mighty *ferment.* With its teeming millions, its diverse races, its castes and outcastes, its princes in palaces and its beggars in hovels, its philosophers in yellow robes and its holy men on beds of spikes, with a civilization reaching back five thousand years into a dim and distant past—this ancient land of India, after the long sleep of centuries, is waking to new life today and girding herself with new strength.

In the providence of God, the Hindu mind, keen and versatile as ever, brought into contact with the free spirit of the West, has felt the stirring of a new life. The schools and colleges of India are crowded with students, no longer poring over the dusty pages of Sanskrit books but eagerly absorbing Western science and learning. Fifteen thousand graduates are passing out of Indian universities every year and one hundred and fifty thousand students are enrolled in her colleges. The Calcutta University has in its affiliated colleges more students than Harvard, Yale and Princeton combined. These young men, educated on Western lines, speaking the English language perfectly, are becoming thoroughly imbued with modern political, social and religious ideas. In science, in law, in medicine, in engineering, in journalism and in statecraft they are distinguishing themselves. A few years ago an Indian student came out Senior Wrangler at Cambridge University and is now principal of Fergusson College, Bombay. Three million Hindus today speak the English language. The Indian National Congress, the most powerful political party in India, holds its deliberations in English. Only thus could the Punjabi, the Bengali, the Madrassi and all the rest meet on a common platform. The English language has become one of the most powerful unifying forces in India and is rapidly becoming the medium of expression for New India.

Democratic ideas, now swiftly spreading throughout the

world, are finding congenial soil and a ready response in the hearts of the educated classes in India. With this awakening to new life has come a growing consciousness of nationality and an insistant demand for independence. The vision of India taking her place side by side with Canada, Australia and South Africa as a free and self-governing dominion in the British commonwealth of nations (or even as an absolutely independent nation) seized the imagination and fired the hearts of the leaders who made bold to declare that nothing less than this could ever satisfy India.

In the realm of religion no more striking figure has appeared in the East for a century than that of the great Bengali reformer, Keshub Chandar Sen (one of the founders of the *Bramho Samaj* and a pioneer of Social Reform) who flashed across the Eastern sky like a meteor. And most significant of all, in these last days India has given to the world two imperishable names—Rabindra Nath Tagore, Bengali poet and winner of the Nobel Prize, and Mahatma Gandhi, a frail little man in a loin cloth, arousing his people, not by the sword but by the power of "soul-force," to a mighty struggle for freedom. In our report of 1922 we said:

> Things are moving rapidly in India. Great changes are taking place before our eyes. New and powerful forces are at work in this ancient land, sweeping away old landmarks, uprooting old customs, liberating the life of the people. Without doubt the next few years will be crucial, soul-stirring, momentous years in the life of this people. India faces a grave situation. No one can tell what a day may bring forth. It may be in a baptism of blood that India will take her place among the self-governing peoples of the earth, or it may be by slow and painful evolution, step by step, as contemplated in the Resolution of 1917. However it may come, one thing is sure: A **NEW INDIA** is rising on the foundations of the old, greater and grander than the India of the past.

Democracy in the East

Now what does this new India want? This new India

wants *freedom;* she wants to govern herself; she wants to see the last Englishman leave her shores. If you would understand this revolutionary movement, you must get the historical background. You must remember that it was Great Britain that taught India this lesson. For a century and a half, through her schools and colleges modeled on Western lines, her free institutions and laws, her system of equal justice and enlightened administration, Great Britain has been teaching India the art of self-government. In the fertile soil of the East she has sown the seeds of democracy and inculcated the ideas of liberty, equality and fraternity. These ideas germinated. A tremendous impetus was imparted to the movement by the first great war, in which Indian troops fought side by side with British soldiers on the fields of France and Egypt and Mesopotamia, shedding their blood in the common cause. In that great crisis of human history India demonstrated on the battlefield her loyalty to the king-emperor. In recognition of India's service and in line with past constitutional development, on August 20, 1917, the secretary of state for India made his famous declaration in Parliament:

> "The policiy of His Majesty's government is that of the increasing association of Indians in every branch of the administration and the gradual development of self-governing institutions with a view to the progressive realization of responsible government in India as an integral part of the British Empire."

This announcement of government was hailed with delight by the Indian people and was justly regarded as a new *Magna Carta* for India. Step by step, in the Montagu Chelmsford Reforms introduced in 1919 and in the Sir John Simon Commission of 1927, the government sought to carry out this policy, but these reforms failed to satisfy Indian aspirations. Finally in 1930 the government called a Round Table Conference in London. Composed of delegates from

British India, rulers of the Indian states and members of Parliament, all sitting on an equality, its purpose was the consideration of the Indian constitutional problem. It was opened amid scenes of great splendor by the king-emperor, and presided over by the prime minister. The Indian constitutional problem, however, proved to be so complex and baffling that one conference was not sufficient and between 1930 and 1933 no less than three Round Table Conferences were held. On the basis of the recommendations of these conferences, in 1933 the government presented a draft constitution for India. In the historic debate in the House of Commons that ensued, Stanley Baldwin, then prime minister, sounded this warning to his countrymen: "Today you have a good chance of keeping India forever in the Empire. If you refuse her this opportunity for self-government, you will inevitably lose India before two generations are passed." His warning was heeded and after a momentous debate, the Bill was passed in the Act of 1935, giving India a new Constitution.

This Constitution, in many respects similar to our own, calls for an All India Federation, or, as we would say, a United States of India—the Federation to consist of the eleven provinces of British India and the Indian states, the provinces and the states to be autonomous, having full control of all internal affairs. In 1937, after a general election, this constitution came into effect in British India. The provinces became fully self-governing with their own premiers and legislatures. The princes, however, were still hesitating to come into the scheme.

Britain's Offer of Independence

Then came the war. Things moved rapidly. Japan in her victorious march from Singapore to Burma stood at the gates of India. The whole-hearted co-operation of India in the war became of vital concern to the allied cause. Faced with this situation, the British government offered India full and complete independence, *"immediately hostilities are ended."* In March, 1942, Sir Stafford Cripps was sent to India to carry out the necessary negotiations with the Indian leaders.

On March 23 Cripps arrived in New Delhi with high hopes of a settlement of the Indian problem. After a week of preliminary discussion with representative Indian leaders, on March 29 Cripps released the British offer in a broadcast to the Indian people. As to the object in view, he said:

> "We wanted to make it quite clear and without any possibility of doubt or question that the British government and the British people desire the Indian peoples to have full self-government, with a constitution as free in every respect as our own in Great Britain, or as of any of the great dominion members of the British commonwealth of nations. In the words of the draft declaration, the British defines its object as, "The creation of a new Indian Union which shall constitute a Dominion, associated with the United Kingdom and the other dominions by a common allegiance to the Crown, but equal to them in every respect, in no way subordinate in any aspect of its domestic or external affairs.
>
> "The principle on which these provisions are based is that the new constitution should be framed by the elected representatives of the Indian people themselves. So we propose that immediately hostilities are ended a constitution-making body should be set up, consisting of elected representatives from British India and, if the states agree to this, as we hope they will, to become part of the Union, they too will be invited to send representatives to this constitution-making body."

This is the substance of this historic document. In closing his eloquent and moving address Cripps made a powerful appeal to the Indian people:

> "I personally am convinced of the soundness and completeness of these proposals. There will still be difficulties, perhaps, the result of distrust that has grown up between us in past years, but I ask you to turn your back upon that past and to accept our hand of

friendship and trust and to allow us to join with you, for the time being, in working to establish and complete your freedom. Regrets and recriminations as to the past can have no place beside the tasks of the future, when a free India will take her rightful place as a co-worker with the other free nations in that world-reconstruction which alone can make the toil and suffering of the war worth while. Let us march together side by side through the night of high endeavour and courage to the already waking dawn of a new world of liberty for all people."

Rejection of the Offer

One would have thought that these stirring and appealing words from a great friend of India would have brought an immediate and whole-hearted response to such an unprecedented offer. Here was what India had long been asking—*full and complete independence, with the right to frame her own constitution by her own chosen representatives.* Unfortunately India could not forget the past and turn her back upon it, as Cripps had urged, and the Indian leaders could not agree among themselves. The Indian National Congress, led by Mahatma Gandhi, demanded *immediate* independence and that with Japan at the gates of India. On the other hand, the Moslem League, representing ninety milion Mohammedans, led by Mohammed Ali Jinnah, demanded a separate Moslem state, formed of the provinces in which there was a Moslem majority, thus dividing India into Hindu and Moslem states. It was the old, old conflict between the Hindu and the Moslem which caused so much bitterness and strife in the past. On the rock of Indian disunity and distrust the negotiations broke down.

On April 11, with the rejection of his proposals by the Indian National Congress and the Moslem League, Cripps's mission came to an end in an atmosphere of gloom. "With the enemy at the gates," Cripps said, his proposals had met with "a critical and unconstructive attitude" on the part of Indian leaders. But with noble magnanimity he said: "I have not lost hope that the people of India will one day come to an agreement. I have no idea when it will be. It depends upon the Indians themselves—on the Indian parties and the Indian leaders. We offered them everything we could. There was nothing more to offer."

Congress Ultimatum to Britain

After the failure of the Cripps mission, as the imminence of invasion by Japan grew more intense day by day, the situation rapidly deteriorated. On August 5, the Working Committee of the Indian National Congress, in a twelve hundred word resolution, demanded the *"withdrawal of British power"* from India, threatening that if Britain rejected the demand for Indian independence, a civil disobedience movement would be launched. On the following day, in the *London Times,* Sir Stafford Cripps predicted chaos in India if Britain should meet the demand of Gandhi and the Indian National Congress for complete withdrawal from India.

Gandhi's Arrest

In the face of the Congress threat, the Indian government acted swiftly and decisively. On August 9, 1942, Gandhi and the Congress leaders were arested. Gandhi was interned in the Aga Khan's palace in Poona. Rioting broke out in Bombay and in many other cities. Shops were looted, buses and street cars smashed. Telegraph and telephone wires were cut and trains were wrecked. Property was destroyed to the extent of many million pounds. Gandhi's "non-violent" campaign soon became intensely violent, as always in the past. To restore order the police fired on the rioting mobs and in some cases machine-gunned the crowds. But the prompt action of the government in arresting the leaders nipped the movement in the bud. Law and order was restored and the attempt to paralyze the government ended in failure.

Gandhi Released

After twenty-one months of imprisonment in the Aga Khan's palace, Gandhi was released on May 6, 1944. The government released him unconditionally, "solely" on the ground of his grave illness. Evidently the government did not want him to die in confinement, thus becoming a martyr to Indian freedom. The press, of all shades of opinion, British as well as Nationalist, acclaimed the release of the seventy-four year old Nationalist leader. Released with Gandhi were Dr. M. D. Gilder, who attended him in detention, and Miss Madaline Slade, the daughter of an English admiral and life-long disciple. Gandhi's release was attended without marked demonstration, but crowds gathered at the palace gates to greet him. He looked cheerful but tired and was taken at once to "Parnakuti", palatial residence of Lady Vitall Das Thakensey, an old friend of Gandhi.

In the twenty-one months since that fateful day of August 9, 1942, when Gandhi launched his civil disobedience campaign in a final desperate effort to win independence for India, conditions had vastly changed—not only in India, but in the world. The threat of invasion by Japan had passed. The Allied cause was everywhere triumphant. India had become a vast "arsenal of democracy" in the East and Britain was more powerful than ever. However, though the Congress leaders were still languishing behind prison walls, the fires of the revolutionary movement had not died out. One day the flame of freedom would burst forth anew.

Gandhi—Jinnah Talks

One of the most influential Hindu leaders in India today,

recognized as the keenest intellect in the Congress party, is Chakravarthi Rajagopalachari (familiarily called by his followers "C. R.") former Premier of the Madras Presidency. His brilliant administration of that great province marked him as one of India's outstanding leaders. Though an intimate friend of Gandhi and one of his devoted followers, when Cripps came to India with the British offer of independence "C. R." strongly advocated acceptance of the proposals. He finally resigned from the India National Congress on its adoption of Gandhi's policy of "non-violent non-co-operation" in the face of the threatened invasion of India by Japan. After the outbreak of the war "C. R." became an unwavering advocate of all-out Indian effort against Japan, and was the only one of the Congress leaders who was not interned. Furthermore, he consistantly advocated Hindu-Moslem agreement as essential to the attainment of India's independence, and even endorsed the claim of the Moslem League for a separate Moslem state. While a firm believer in the essential unity of India and strongly opposed to Ali Jinnah's proposal of Pakistan he clearly saw that under a free constitution such as India was seeking, provinces or states must be free to accept or reject federal union. "Independence", he said, "must be built up of consenting units, if it is to rest, not on outward force, but on abiding cohesive strength. If we cannot agree among ourselves to form one central government, it is surely better for the growth of freedom and democracy in this vast country that those who insist on a separate existance should be allowed to try it out." This position he strongly urged upon Congress leaders after the rejection of the Cripps proposals, but Congress was absolutely opposed to any break in Indian unity.

On the release of Gandhi it was evident that something must be done. As soon as the aged leader regained his strength "C. R." urged upon him the necessity of a Hindu-Moslem agreement in order to break the deadlock in Indian political affairs, and finally won Gandhi to his side. His proposal was that a commission be appointed to demarcate contiguous districts in the Northwest and East India, where the Moslem population was a majority. In the areas thus demarcated a plebiscite of the inhabitants should be held to determine whether or not they desired a separate Moslem state. On the basis of this formula, on September 9, 1944, Gandhi and Ali Jinnah began their talks in an attempt to solve the political differences between the Hindus and Mohammedans. After eighteen days of negotiations, however, they failed to reach an agreement. It was a brave attempt, not without goodwill, but it clearly showed the thorny pathway to reconciliation between Hindus and Mohammedans. With Gandhi assenting to the principle of self-determination as the basis of settlement, one would have thought an agreement possible, but even that concession failed to produce results.

What, then, shall we say to the scheme of *Pakistan?* The difficulties in forming a separate Moslem state in India would seem to be well-nigh insuperable. As Lord Wavell has aptly said, "You cannot alter geography. India is a natural unit." As to the population, of the ninety-two million Mohammedans in India nearly one-half or forty per cent are outside the proposed Pakistan State. Hyderabad, the most powerful Mohammedan state in India, is in the South, far removed from Pakistan. Of the four provinces in Northwest and East India in which Moslems are in a majority, Punjab, Sind and the northwest frontier provinces form a contiguous area, but between them and Bengal lie two great provinces predominently Hindu, stretching a thousand miles in extent. Furthermore, in the heart of the Punjab are five million Sikhs, a fighting race, bitterly opposed to Moslem rule. Finally, the Moslem League did not by any means represent all Mohammedans, many being members of the Congress party.

These were stubborn facts for Ali Jinnah, but in spite of them he seemed determined to have his Moslem state at all costs.

Wavell Breaks the Dead-Lock

On June 18, 1943, the British government announced the appointment of Field Marshal Sir Archibald Wavell, British Commander in Chief in India, as viceroy and governor general of India to succeed Lord Linlithgow on his retirement in October. The appointment of a soldier to be viceroy was unprecedented and came as a great surprise, but was welcomed by all parties as a masterly stroke. As one of Great Britain's most brilliant military leaders and as a statesman of farsighted vision and great ability, it was felt that Lord Wavell was eminently fitted for the high position. Furthermore, he had first-hand knowledge of India. As commander in chief of the army he was a member of the Viceroy's Council. During the discussions with Indian leaders he was in close touch with Sir Stafford Cripps and was known to be in sympathy with Indian political aspirations. With such a man, not a "hardened politician" but a soldier-statesman, at the helm there was hope of a fresh approach to the Indian problem.

On October 18 at New Delhi, Viscount Wavell was enstalled Viceroy of India. In a simple ceremony, without pageant or parade, he mounted the throne of the mightiest empire in the East, becoming the ruler of four hundred million people. He was fundamentally a soldier and he cared not for pomp or ceremony. Mingling freely with the people, he visited every province in India to get first-hand knowledge of conditions. When he took the reins of government, famine was sweeping over vast areas of India and hundreds of people were daily dying in the streets of Calcutta. At once he went in person to the affected areas and took immediate steps to relieve distress. In his first address to the Indian Central

Legislature at Delhi, on February 19, 1944, he boldly took his stand on the question of the independence of India. He said:

> "Nearly two years have passed since the Cripps Draft Declaration was made public, but it stands forth today as the solemn pledge of His Majesty's government that India shall have full control of her own destiny along with the nations of the commonwealth and the world . . . I am a sincere friend of India and I should like to help her to political advance, but my military training has made me quite certain that no objective is ever gained without the fullest co-operation from all concerned."

After eighteen months of intensive study of India's problems, Wavell became convinced that steps must be taken to break the Indian deadlock and that he must act. Accordingly he flew to London to confer with the British government. He found the British leaders engrossed in the prosecution of the war. "Why trouble me with this business now?," said Churchill. "Can't you wait?" "No," said Wavell. Britain had pledged her word that India should have self-government; she must keep her word. Congress leaders were languishing in jail. The situation was drifting dangerously. The deadlock must be broken. Without a new offer from the government, he would not return to India at all. That nailed it. His plan was passed.

In accordance with Wavell's plan, on June 15, 1945, the British government offered India increased participation in the government and renewed its 1942 proposal for post-war dominion status for India. Under this plan the Viceroy's Council (Cabinet) would be composed entirely of Indians, except for the viceroy and the commander in chief, "on a balanced representation of the main communities, including equal proportions of Moslems and Hindus." Foreign Affairs, now controlled by the viceroy, would pass into Indian hands, as well as Finance and Home Department. Indians would thus hold all posts in the Cabinet, except that of Defence under Sir Claude Auchenleck, Commander in Chief. At the same time, in a broadcast from New Delhi to the Indian people Viscount Wavell announced the release of eight members of the Congress party's Working Committee who were still in custody; and issued an invitation to leaders of Indian political parties to meet him at Simla, June 25, to consider these proposals. In a message to the viceroy Gandhi said he would use his influence with the Working Committee to accept the proposals. The Moslem press generally welcomed the British offer. Bombay despatches said all sections of Indian public opinion felt the British proposals placed India at least within sight of dominion status.

The Simla Conference

On June 25, as announced, the leaders of Indian political parties met with Viscount Wavell at Simla to consider the British proposals. The conference met in a spirit of goodwill which augured well for the success of the deliberations. The Congress leaders expressed their willingness to cooperate and take office, but Ali Jinnah and the Moslem League rejected the Wavell proposals, taking an uncompromising stand on Pakistan, the proposed Moslem state. In view of the opposition, Viscount Wavell decided not to proceed further with the plan and generously took upon himself the blame for the failure. In closing the conference he said: "I propose to take a little time to consider in what way I can best help India."

The Simla Conference, though not attaining its complete goal, was by no means a failure. The Congress leaders, so long imprisoned, were liberated and called into council. By its offer of an enlarged Viceroy's Council, composed entirely of Indians with the exception of the viceroy and the commander-in-chief, the British government had shown its determination to press on toward the goal of full self-government for India. The long and barren deadlock was broken and the door was now open to future developments which came swiftly in the wake of the victory of the Labor party in Britain.

The Dominion of India

On taking office August 5, 1945, the Labor government pledged itself to the "early realization of full self-government in India." In fulfillment of that pledge, on September 19, in simultaneous broadcasts, Prime Minister Clement Attlee from London and Viceroy Viscount Wavell from New Delhi, presented the Labor government's solution of the baffling Indian problem. Based on Sir Stafford Cripps's scheme of 1942, with modifications, the plan proposed as follows:

1. A general election to the Central Assembly and the eleven provincial legislatures to take place between November 1945 and the spring of 1946.
2. After the election, steps will be taken to set up a Constituent Assembly of Indian elected representatives, charged with the task of framing a new constitution for India.
3. The Indian states will be invited to take part in the scheme.
4. The viceroy is authorized to take steps to bring into being an executive council having the support of the main Indian parties.
5. Finally, the British government will draft a treaty to be concluded between the government of Great Britain and the Dominion of India safeguarding the rights of minorities.

In these proposals, it will be seen, definite and positive steps were prescribed to bring into being full and complete self-government in India, both in the provinces and at the center, and to frame a constitution by representatives duly chosen by the people, the Indian states also being invited to join the scheme. This was essentially the Cripps plan, of which

C. Rajagopalachari said; "The British government could not offer a scheme going further than that embodied in the Cripps proposals on the point of national independence." Here, then, we have broad and constructive proposals for a *Federated India* or, as we would say, a *United States of India,* composed of the provinces of British India and the Indian states, the whole constituting *The Dominion of India.*

It is well to remember, however, that this great scheme of nation-building could not be successfully carried through to completion without the co-operation of the Indian people. Prime Minister Attlee in his broadcast to the Indian people sounded this solemn note:

> "No one who has any acquaintance with Indian affairs will underestimate the difficulties which have to be surmounted. During the war, Indian fighting men have played a splendid part in defeating the forces of tyranny and aggression. I ask all Indians to follow their great example and to join in a united effort to work out a constitution which majority and minority communities will accept as just and fair."

The viceroy, Field-Marshall Viscount Wavell, in an eloquent address on "*Indian Problems of Today and Tomorrow,*" delivered before the Indian Central Legislature in New Delhi, February 17, 1944, made this moving appeal to his Indian friends:

> "We have come a long way together, up a steep and difficult mountain at the summit of which lies complete Indian self-government. We are almost within sight of the top but, as with most mountain climbs that are worth doing, the final cliffs are the steepest and most baffling of all. At such a time it is doubly necessary to test each handhold and foothold, to cut adequate steps in the slippery ice so that the whole party roped together may not fall back in ruin. It is not the moment that prudent mountaineers choose to unrope, to dismiss their guides and, after violent dispute, to take separate routes toward different peaks. We must go on together. We cannot halt too long at the heights which we have reached, and we cannot with honor or safety turn back. Finally, we must keep

in mind the splendor of the view that lies before us when the summit is reached. The prospect of India at peace within herself, a partner in our great commonwealth of nations, the mother of a great people, a shield for peace in the East, busy and prosperous, yet with leisure to develop thought and poetry and art which are the real salt of life and of which India has already contributed so much to the world—this not an unattainable vision, if we work together with patience, good sense and good will."

These were noble words from the heart of a sincere friend of India, an inspiring vision of India's great future—a vision that was gloriously fulfilled in a few short years.

Very shortly after this, another step was taken in the amazing drama of India. On February 19, 1946, Prime Minister Attlee announced in the House of Commons that the British government had decided to send out to India a special mission of Cabinet ministers to assist Indian leaders in the task of framing a new constitution for India. The ministers constituting this mission were Sir Stafford Cripps, President of the Board of Trade, Lord Pethick-Lawrence, Secretary of State for India, and A. V. Alexander, First Lord of the Admiralty. It was eminently fitting that Sir Stafford Cripps, author of the "Cripps Plan" for Indian independence in 1942, should head this mission and carry through to completion the great task which he then undertook.

On the eve of the departure of the Cabinet ministers on this weighty mission to India, on March 15, Prime Minister Attlee in a challenging speech in the House of Commons, offering India *complete independence, whether in the British Empire or out of it,* made this historic declaration:

"India must choose as to what will be her future constitution and what will be her position in the world. I hope that the Indian people may elect to remain within the British commonwealth of nations. But if India does so elect, it must be her own free will. The British Commonwealth is not bound together by chains of external compulsion. It is a free association of free peoples. If, on the other hand, India elects for independence, in our view, she has the right to do so. It will be for us to make the transition as smooth and easy as possible."

"Finally, I would stress the crucial nature of the task before us. This is a problem of vital importance not only to India and the British Empire, but to the world . . . Here is a great country which has been seeking to apply the principles of democracy, and I myself have always hoped that politically India might be the light of Asia. The ministers are going out to India resolved to succeed and I am sure that every one will wish them Godspeed."

India wins her Freedom

From this time on things began to move rapidly. Owing to differences with the home government in respect to the Indian question, on February 20, 1947, Viceroy Lord Wavell resigned and Admiral Viscount Mountbatten, a great-grandson of the first Empress of India, Queen Victoria, was chosen to be the last viceroy of India, bringing to a close two centuries of British rule over the vast sub-continent of India.

On that same date, Prime Minister Attlee announced in the House of Commons the decision of the British government to withdraw completely from India not later than June, 1948. This decision of the British government was acclaimed throughout India. Pundit Jawaharlal Nehru, leader of the Indian Congress party, pronounced it a "wise and courageous act, a challenge to all of us." Mahatma Gandhi termed it "the noblest act of the British nation."

On taking the oath of office which made him Governor-General of India, with rare tact and skill and deep understanding of the Indian problem, Lord Mountbatten addressed himself to the task before him. "I am under no illusion about the difficulty of my task," he said. "I shall need the greatest good will of the greatest possible number and I am asking India for that good will."

All efforts, however, to bring the Hindus and Moslems together in a central government, preserving the unity of

India, proved unavailing. The tension between the two peoples increased from day to day and finally broke out in open riot and bloodshed. The only solution seemed to be the partition of India into Hindu and Moslem states, each having the status of a dominion. After prolonged conferences with Indian leaders of all parties and heart-to-heart discussions with Mohammed Ali Jinnah, President of the Moslem League, Pandit Jawaharlal Nehru, leader of the All-India Congress party and Mohandas K. Gandhi, the spiritual leader of India, Mountbatten became convinced that the Hindus and Mohammedans could not be held together and that the formation of a central government was impossible. Finally he was summoned to London to present his views to the British Cabinet.

As the result of the discussions with Lord Mountbatten, on June 3, 1947, Prime Minister Attlee, in an historic address, laid before the House of Commons a plan to *partition* India into Moslem and Hindu states, each having the status of a dominion. Simultaneously a similar statement was addressed to the Indian people by the viceroy in New Delhi.

The plan was welcomed not only by the government supporters in the House of Commons, but even by Winston Churchill, Conservative opposition leader in the House. As millions heard the voice of the viceroy in his broadcast to the nation, presenting the plan proposed by the government, and the messages of their leaders, Mohammed Ali Jinnah, Jawaharlal Nehru and Mahatma Gandhi, accepting the plan, a wave of relief and joy swept over India in the realization that peace had at last come to the troubled land. Writing of this historic event in his column in the *Herald-Tribune* of June 7, 1947, Walter Lippman pays a high tribute to Britain:

> Perhaps Britain's finest hours are not in the past. Certainly this performance is not the work of a decadent people. This, on the con-

trary, is a work of political genius, requiring the ripest wisdom and the freshest vigor, and it is done with an elegance and a style that will compel and will receive an instinctive respect throughout the civilized world.

On August 15, 1947, at midnight, amid the ringing of bells, the blowing of horns and the cheers of millions of jubilant men, women and children all over India, the Union Jack was hauled down and in its place was raised the orange, white and green banner of the *Dominion of India* and the white and green flag of *Pakistan*—marking the passing of the British Raj and the birth of two new nations. In this historic event, brought to pass in a bloodless revolution, were fulfilled the hopes and dreams of India's patriots and sages through long and bitter centuries. In the fullness of the times, under the guiding hand of God, India has taken her rightful place among the free peoples of the earth.

The Outlook for Christianity

What, then, is the outlook for Christianity in a free India? Some view the future with fear and apprehension. Now that the protecting hand of Great Britain is removed, what will be the fate of Christian missions? Having seized the reins, will India tolerate propaganda? Will not the proud spirit of the *Brahman* assert itself and sweep away the last vestage of the white man's religion? Such thoughts are born of fear.

In the first place, it must be remembered that after two centuries of struggle, Christianity is now firmly planted in the soil of India. It is no longer an exotic. The seed has been sown far and wide. Already there is a mighty harvest. With nine million converts won from every race and caste and religion in this great land, with schools and colleges for the education and training of Christian leaders, with a vast army of Indian workers set apart to Christian service and pushing out into every bazaar and market-place, with an Indian church strong and aggressive, rapidly growing in self-support and self-determination, Christianity is well prepared to take her place as a vital force in the life of a new India.

Nor is this all. Far beyond numerical strength, outward organization and external forms, the leaven of Christianity has been working now for two centuries, silently and irrestibily in the hearts of the people and it has wrought a revolution. The Bible has now become one of the sacred books of the Hindus and our Christ, one of their *Avatars* (Incarnations). In the past Christianity has been handicapped by the dominance of the foreigner. It has been tied, so to speak, to a Western power and entangled in the meshes of Western civilization. Freed from this bondage, we may expect Christianity to move on to new victories and to lay still deeper hold on the mind and heart of India.

In the second place, Christianity has always stood for freedom. Freedom is the very air she breathes. In every land and among every people Christianity has befriended the down-trodden and the oppressed and struck off the shackles of the slave. As Christians, therefore, and followers of Him who came to set men free, we cannot fail to sympathize with this great people in their aspirations for liberty and self-government. We must wish them well. We must stand by as friends and helpers. We welcome India on attainment of her birth-right as a free and self-governing people. As such we greet a free India. In the uprising of this great people we see the providence of God. We see India taking her place among the nations of the earth—a free and independent people. And in the long and arduous struggle that lies before her, we believe that she needs most of all the guiding hand of God and the uplifting and transforming power of Christ.

II

THE CALL OF INDIA

From this ancient land, now waking to new life and conscious of new power, there came to a man in the days gone by a *CALL,* loud and clear, as from God. The closing years of the last century witnessed one of the most remarkable movements in the religious life of America—a great missionary uprising among the students of American colleges. Born in a students' conference at Mount Hermon, Massachusetts, July 1886, it was led by Robert P. Wilder, John N. Forman and Robert E. Speer, an outstanding group of Princeton students, and John R. Mott of Cornell. Taking as its watchword *"The Evangelization of the World in this Generation,"* the Student Volunteer Movement for Foreign Missions swept over American colleges and thousands of students dedicated their lives to foreign mission service.

At the height of this movement in the fall of 1889, Robert E. Speer, the travelling secretary, came to Colgate University, Hamilton, New York. I was then a student there, just graduated from college and in the first year of my seminary course. I well remember the great meeting of the whole student body (college, academy and seminary) held that night in the academy chapel when Speer made his powerful appeal to the students to dedicate their lives to God and to the cause of foreign missions. At that time I had not the remotest idea of foreign missions. Though my father was a minister and though I had resolved to follow in his footsteps, my vision of Christian service had never reached beyond the bounds of my own country. Even Speer's powerful appeal might have fallen on dull ears had it not been for one compelling fact. Recently I had passed through a profound spiritual experience. In my Junior year in college a beautiful, gifted and charming young lady, Fanny Elizabeth Forward by name, came across my path and completely won my heart. The love in my heart for this sweet girl created a mighty spiritual upheaval, stirring me to the very depths of my being. I became, as it were, a new man—transformed by the love for this woman. In that hour Speer came with his mighty summons to sacrifice, his ringing call to *follow Christ to the ends of the earth.* It came as the voice of God to my soul and that very night, in the old academy chapel, with bowed head and tears streaming down my face, I surrendered to God. I heard the voice of the Lord saying, "Whom shall I send and who will go for us?"

I answered, "Here am I, Lord, send *me*."

Very soon after that memorable night, I disclosed the secret to my betrothed. Not without some trepidation of heart I told her of my decision. Without a moment's hesitation and with shining face she said, "Where you go, I will follow." That night, in the little "sky parlor" in Bouckville, her home, we sealed our vows to God and to each other.

Shortly after this I was sent as a delegate from Colgate to the Student Volunteer Convention which was held that year at Cleveland, Ohio. Under the inspiration of those great meetings in which Robert E. Speer and John R. Mott were the moving spirits, the call of India sounded louder and louder in my ears.

India now became the all-absorbing thought in my life. On the wall of my room in old Eaton Hall I hung a great map of India and day and night I kept before me the vision of that great land in its darkness and destitution. All the books on India that I could find were eagerly read. The missionary interest in Colgate deepened from day to day.

The volunteer band grew to over fifty members. Under the auspices of the band monthly missionary meetings were held in the Hamilton Baptist Church and student bands on India, China, Japan and Africa were sent out to kindle the fires of missionary zeal in the hearts of the people.

In June, 1892, I graduated from the seminary, my chum "Pete" Guernsey and myself being the two volunteers in our class. That summer I went as a delegate to the Northfield Student Volunteer Conference, where representatives from all the Eastern colleges in U. S. A. were present. Missionary enthusiasm reached a high pitch and in the "Round Top" meetings and under the trees of the beautiful campus many a man with Bible in hand fought out the battle with self and made the great surrender.

Marriage and Ordination

On September 6, 1892, in the old home at Bouckville, New York, Fanny and I were married. The little "sky parlor" where we had courted in times past and where we had made our vows to each other, was banked with goldenrod and ferns gathered from the woods near by, a fresh and lovely sight. My father performed the wedding ceremony, assisted by Rev. Dewitt Forward, Fanny's elder brother. The Colgate boys, my college pals, and Fanny's Y. L. R. S. girls from Hamilton formed the happy group that gathered about us and cheered us on our shining way.

On September 15, a few days after our wedding, I was ordained in the Baptist church at Hamilton, New York, my old college town. The late Dr. William Newton Clarke, my beloved teacher in the seminary to whom I owed so much in my spiritual life, preached the ordination sermon. He took as his text Isaiah 40:3—"Prepare ye in the wilderness a highway for our God." His theme was, *"Road-builders for the King."* Even now, after the lapse of fifty years, I can hear his clarion call summoning me to build a highway in the wilderness for the coming of the King. With the prayer of Dedication offered by my sainted father, the solemn service came to a close. It was a hallowed and sacred hour in my life.

Sailing for India

September was a great month for us. On the sixth we were married, on the fifteenth I was ordained and on the twenty-fourth we sailed for India. A honeymoon trip to India! How wonderful! How glorious! And such it was. We sailed from Boston on the old cattle ship, S. S. "Pavonia" bound for Liverpool. A great farewell meeting was held in one of the largest churches in Boston. Father and Mother Stanton were there to bid us good-bye and *bon voyage.* Very tenderly they took us down into the little cabin set apart for us on board ship and there we knelt together in prayer and wept as they offered us up to God. In our party sailing that day there were sixteen missionaries as follows: Rev. and Mrs. A. H. Curtis, the latter a daughter of Dr. John E. Clough, returning to the land of her birth; Rev. and Mrs. W. S. Davis; Rev. and Mrs. John Dussman; Rev. and Mrs. D. S. Bagshaw; Rev. and Mrs. W. A. Stanton; Rev. and Mrs. Samuel Perrine, bound for Assam; "Judge" F. H. Levering; Rev. P. B. Guernsey; Mrs. Oscar R. McKay and Miss Susan Kurtz—the largest party of Baptist missionaries ever to sail from America for the foreign field. Rev. and Mrs. Wheeler Boggess had already sailed and on October 8 another party of five sailed; Rev. C. R. Marsh, Rev. T. P. Dudley and Rev. and Mrs. W. E. Hopkins in company with Rev. R. Maplesden, returning to his work in the Deccan.

All of us in this party, with the exception of the Perrines, were bound for the old Lone Star Mission in response to the appeal of Dr. John E. Clough for twenty-five missionary families to gather in the great harvest among the Telugus.

Crossing the Atlantic in a frightful storm, Fanny was deathly sick. We called in the ship's doctor and when he heard that we were bound for India he turned to me and said very sternly, "Young man, you are taking your wife to her death. She will never live to see India." But the doctor did not know. An unseen Hand was guiding us. Not only did the frail little wife survive the storms of the Atlantic and the perils of the deep, but by the grace of God she was privileged to give to India forty years of devoted service. "He shall give his angels charge over thee to keep thee, lest at any time thou dash thy foot against a stone."

After a few days in England, seeing the sights of London and making necessary purchases for our life in the East, we sailed on the old British India liner, S. S. *"Taroba"*, a ship so old and unseaworthy that ofttimes we despaired of ever reaching our destination. It was a thrilling journey. We were astonished to find the steamer crowded with young Engishmen in all ranks of life— merchants, lawyers, tea-planters, business-men, India civil servants, government officials. All were going out to India to seek their fortunes! We had thought that only missionaries would be on board ship; that only missionaries would cross the seas. But strange to say these men too had heard the call of the East, only it was another and a different call from ours. As I thought it over in the quiet hours of the voyage, I said to myself, "If these men can leave fair England and cross the seas for material gain and for worldly power and position, it is a very small thing for me, servant of the Living God, to follow my Lord to the ends of the earth!"

Madras to Bapatla

On November 7, after a six weeks' voyage, we landed in

Madras and received a most hearty welcome from the Hadleys, our missionaries stationed there. From Madras we went to Nellore, the old Lone Star station, where we received a royal welcome by the Downies and the Telugu Christians. There we met "Julia", one of that little band of five who, on New Year's morning, 1854, climbed Prayer Meeting Hill as the sun was rising over the hills and knelt and prayed as Father Jewett poured out his soul in prayer for the salvation of the Telugus. With the tears streaming down her face she told the wonderful story. That day in Nellore as we looked for the first time into the happy faces of the Telugu converts and heard their cheery words of welcome, our hearts were deeply stirred and we were glad that we had come to India. It was fitting that the first Telugu word we learned was *santoshum,* (joy) for that was to be the key-note of our service in India.

From Nellore we were to go to Ramapatnam, the seat of our theological seminary, a distance of forty-five miles. As there was no railway along the east coast in those early days, we went by ox-cart. To accommodate our big missionary party, we had a dozen or more carts, two-wheeled affairs covered with bamboo mats and drawn not by oxen but by coolies. A plentiful supply of straw was placed in the bottom of the carts to form a bed and into this we crawled as best we could, two in a cart, with our luggage packed about us. To avoid the heat of the day we made the journey by night. And what a night it was! The long line of carts formed an imposing array. The coolies jogged along at a lively pace and, going down hill as we often did, the carts would bump into each other with a tremendous crash, the coolies would shout and jabber wildly in a strange tongue and we inside would go shunting almost out of the cart. Along the road Fanny spied some lovely plume grass and insisted that I get out and gather some. It was indeed beautiful, but when we crawled out of the cart in the morning at Ramapatnam we had feathered out with a gorgeous coating of plumes!

The Sabbath was spent at Ramapatnam, the "School of the Prophets" by the sea. In the cool of the morning we roamed under the wide-spreading branches of the great banyan trees that adorned the beautiful campus of a hundred acres. At ten o'clock we gathered for worship in the stately cathedral (built by the veteran missionary, Dr. R. R. Williams) with a hundred and fifty Telugu men and women preparing for the gospel ministry. Joining as best we could in singing the hymns to the weird tunes of Indian music, we heard for the first time in our lives the Gospel of the Son of God preached in an unknown tongue, which one day we fondly hoped would become *our* tongue. That Sunday was a high-day in Zion.

With our arrival at Ramapatnam we had by no means reached our journey's end. Our destination was Bapatla where we were to be stationed for the study of the language, a journey of about one hundred miles and—no railway! While we were wondering how we were to get there, "Willie" Boggs, our missionary at Ramapatnam, informed us that the Bapatla "house boat" had been sent for us and that we were to make the journey by boat on the Buckingham Canal and that he would accompany us. We were wildly excited at the prospect. Many thrills we had had on our voyage from the United States, but this was to be the final "thriller". The house boat was a staunch little craft, fitted out with a good-sized cabin where we had our meals by day and slept by night, a tiny bathroom where you were not expected to bathe, and a kitchen in the stern where the native cook held forth. The boat was flat on top and in the cool of the evening it was delightful to sit "on deck" and watch the changing panorama of trees and hills and sky and waving rice fields, as we glided with scarcely a ripple through the silent waters of the canal. The boat was fitted with a good sail so that when the wind was favorable we could hoist the sail and go dashing up the canal at a pretty good speed. India is the land of manpower. When our ship cast anchor in Madras harbor, coolies came swarming up the sides of the ship, struggling and fighting with each other to take off our luggage; and in the streets of Madras huge carts piled high with goods of every description were drawn not by oxen but by sweating and straining coolies. So our house boat was drawn, not by oxen, but by six or eight stalwart coolies, treading along the canal bank, pulling a long rope attached to the boat, and making about three miles an hour! "Willie" Bogg was our captain and navigator, and ofttimes he would call out to the coolies, *"Pitchayya, jeldi, jeldi!"* which meant in good English, "Crazy man, quickly, quickly." But the "crazyman" quickened his pace not a bit. One of the pretty sights was when native boats laden with rice and carrying huge sails passed us. Invariably, when they sighted us in the distance, they lowered their sails as they passed by. So great was the deference to the *white man.* This striking act brought home to us for the first time a realization of the power and prestige of the British *Raj* in India.

The Buckingham Canal runs parallel to the coast and in many places not far from the sea. We had many rivers to cross and this was ofttimes a dangerous operation. Passing out from the canal into the river, the coolies were put on board and the crew manned the bamboo poles, for now we must be poled across; the river was wide and deep, the waves were rolling in from the sea, the wind was blowing a fierce gale and sometimes we were nearly blown out to sea. After crossing one of these rivers, we found the canal blocked with silt from the river bed, so that boats could not pass. They kept coming down from the upper canal until finally the canal was blocked with two or three hundred boats. Into this mass of struggling humanity and shouting natives we were plunged and caught and for three days were held fast in their grip.

At last we reached our destination—a little native village on the banks of the canal. Bapatla was eight miles away. "Will" Owen, our old friend of Colgate days, now missionary at Bapatla, was there to meet us with a band of schoolboys and their helpers. On every side were broad stretches of rice fields with a vast network of irrigation channels and only a narrow cart path leading to Bapatla. No automobiles were awaiting us, but something far more interesting and picturesque—a palanquin for Fanny, borne by four stalwart coolies, and a native pony for me so diminutive that my feet almost touched the ground as we jogged along. Fanny led off in the palanquin, I was close behind on the pony, and Will and the native band brought up the rear. At the mission bungalow "Beth" Owen and a great crowd of mission workers, preachers, teachers, Bible women and boarding school boys and girls, were assembled to receive us. In true oriental style, we were garlanded with flowers, sprinkled with rose water and presented with limes and betel nut. Welcome songs were sung in Telugu to Telugu music and welcome addresses presented by the Telugu Christians. We had reached our journey's end, ten thousand miles across the seas, and were "at home" in India!

Happy Days in Bapatla

In our first days here it was delightful to be associated with Will and Beth Owen, our old friends in the homeland. A right royal welcome they gave us to their home and many were the happy hours we spent in fellowship with them. They were both musical, Will with his violin and Beth with her sweet voice. Fanny played her guitar and what jolly times we had singing the old college songs! But life was not all singing. Soon we got down to business, the business of learning the Telugu language. At first with a Brahman *munchee* and later on with one of our own Christian teachers we tackled the intricacies of the Telugu tongue and, though often discouraged and disheartened, we made steady progress in the mastery of one of the most difficult languages of the East. Within nine months we had the joy of preaching our first Telugu sermon. And soon we were assigned a task. The Bapatla Mission could boast a strong and vigorous normal training school for our Christian teachers. After a year of language study we were asked to take the Bible lesson with the students of the normal training school. We decided to give them a study in the Parables of Jesus. It was a novel experience to teach the Bible in Telugu, but those first days of meditation and study in the pages of the New Testament with those Telugu students were richly rewarding and long years afterward the echoes came back from those happy days.

On the twenty-fifth of January 1894, two years after our arrival in India, in the right wing of the old Bapatla bungalow which we then called our home, our "Betty" was born. Betty, child of our prayers and dreams, God's first gift in our wedded life. In the birth of this precious child Fanny nearly lost her life—a tragedy which might well have happened, humanly speaking, had it not been for the skill and devotion of a lady missionary doctor, who sat lovingly by her side during those critical hours and brought her safely through. To Doctor Marguerite Armstrong we owe a debt we never can repay. With the coming of this sweet child, once again the floodgates of life were opened and the mighty river of God's love flowed into our souls, bringing life, light and joy.

We were now in our second year in India, able to speak the Telugu language with some degree of freedom and power and, what was more important, we had come to know the people and to love them. Now eagerly and with deep desire we began to think of our future field of service in the Telugu

Mission. We had not long to wait. Soon word came from our Board in Boston that we were designated to *Kurnool,* one of the oldest and most important stations in the Telugu Mission. Our hearts were thrilled as we realized that soon we would have a station of our own and joyfully enter upon the work to which God had called us. We were ready for new tasks.

III

ON THE BANKS OF THE TUNGABHADRA

AFTER two happy years in Bapatla with the Owens and the Telugu Christians, in November 1894 we bade them good-bye and started out with high hopes on the long journey to Kurnool. The first stage was a journey of thirty miles to Guntur, the nearest railroad station. Travelling by night in the little "green coach," drawn by oxen and driven by our faithful bandy-man, we arrived safely the next morning in Guntur. There we took the Southern Maratha train for Dhone (now called Dronachallam) the rail station for Kurnool. The Southern Maratha is a little narrow-gage railroad, constructed in 1876-78 as a famine relief project and running the whole length of the Telugu Mission from Bezvada to Guntakal, a distance of some two hundred and fifty miles. The train could hardly be called a "fast express." Stopping at every station, where the guard and the engineer disappear for a good half hour for a friendly chat and a cup of coffee, the train makes scarcely ten miles an hour. It was a long and tedious journey of a day and a night, relieved only by the picturesque passage through the Nalamalla Hills which rise some 2500 feet above the sea. In the afternoon of the third day we arrived at Dhone, a tiny little station on the Dhone-Kurnool Road.

From Dhone to Kurnool, a distance of thirty-three miles, we travelled by ox-cart, making the journey by night to avoid the heat of the day. With our luggage packed tightly about us and a good bed of straw underneath, Fanny, baby Betty and I were securely, if not comfortably tucked away for the night. We soon found, however, that there were no springs to the cart and no cushions underneath. The road was rough and bumpy. The oxen were unruly, sometimes dashing into the ditch on the side of the road and anon bumping into the carts in front of us. The country was wild and rugged with huge granite boulders looming up in the darkness, the haunts of robbers and wild beasts. The people who passed us on the road looked savage and uncivilized. That night we did not sleep much. Many thoughts about this strange land, so different from what we had expected, came crowding into our minds. In the homeland we had often spoken to eager listeners in the churches about the romance of missions. We had glowingly pictured India with its palm trees, its spices and its "coral strand." But, alas, here we were in a wilderness, bumping over the stones in an ox-cart, dragging along a bleak and dusty road at three miles an hour! No, dear friends, there is no "romance of missions." Foreign missions is a *task,* a heaven-born undertaking, a mighty adventure for God and man—stern and exacting!

In the early dawn we arrived in Kurnool and were given a hearty welcome by Rev. and Mrs. C. N. Thomssen, our Kurnool missionaries. As we climbed out of the old ox-cart, a little band of Telugu Christians greeted us with many salaams and fervent expressions of joy. As we looked into the smiling faces of these Telugu Christians, we were glad that we had come to India.

Kurnool is an old historic town on the banks of the Tungabadhra River, which forms the boundry line between the Hyderabad state on the north and the Kurnool district on the south, 250 miles northwest of Madras and 180 miles west of Ongole. It is the capital of the Kurnool district with a population in those days of some 30,000—nearly half of whom were Mohammedans. Kurnool is a picturesque old town, lying at the junction of the Handri River with the Tungabadhra. In the olden days it was a walled city, and the main bastion which formed part of the wall surrounding the city still stands after five centuries. It is constructed of massive stones fitted together without cement.

The great tomb of Abdul Wahab Khan, the first Mohammedan *Nawab* of Kurnool, built in 1624, is an imposing structure. Its dome rising two hundred feet above the banks of the Handri River, is the most conspicuous object for miles around. In the heart of the town on the main bazaar is the gateway to the palace of *Gopal Raj*, the last Hindu ruler of Kurnool. And near-by is the *Masa Masjit*—a mosque of great sancity in the eyes of Mohammedan worshippers. The foundations and lower wall of this mosque were once part of a Hindu temple. When the Mohammedans took the city they converted the temple into a mosque.

Kurnool is the headquarters of the district. Here are stationed the head officers—the collector, who is the top-ranking officer of the district, the district judge, the police superintendent, the district surgeon in charge of the government hospital, the executive engineer in charge of public works and three district forest officers, administering the extensive forests of the Nalamalla Hills. In the early days when we first went to Kurnool, all of these officers were Britishers with their wives, making a very delightful little colony with its English Club and many social functions, but with the growth of the Nationalist movement and the consequent Indianization of the services, a great change has taken place and today all of the District officers are Indians. Not an Englishman is left—convincing proof of the rapid progress of self-government in India. Kurnool can boast of many fine public buildings, constructed of our beautiful Kurnool limestone—the district court, police headquarters, collector's *Cutchery,* the government hospital with wards for men and women, three high schools and a government

Top: Bastion to the Old Fort, Kurnool. The orange, white and green flag of India now flies from the flag-staff. Center: Our Kurnool home. Bottom: Tomb of Abdul-Wahab Khan, First Nawab of Kurnool, erected 1618.

training school and many fine bungalows. A splendid system of water works provides pure drinking water for all of the inhabitants and, would you believe it, there are electric lights throughout the town in place of the old smoking kerosene lamps. Altogether this is one of the most delightful stations in India.

The Kurnool field—one of the largest in the Telugu Mission—embraces five large *taluks* (counties) and extends 60 miles north and south and 120 miles east and west. It is three times the size of Rhode Island. It has 469 villages with a population of 609,071. Here in America there is a church on well-nigh every corner and sometimes one thrown in between. Out in India your missionary has a field as large as one of our states with a parish of a half-million souls.

Arriving in Kurnool on November 16, 1894, we found ourselves in one of the oldest stations of the Telugu Mission, opened in 1876. Dark and tragic were those early days. In the eighteen years before our arrival, no less than seven missionaries in succession had charge of the work, the average term of service of each being only two and one-half years. Famine swept the land. Sickness depleted the ranks of the missionaries, striking down one after another with the deadly "Kurnool fever." Kurnool was called the *"White Man's Grave"*. Truly foreign missions is a costly enterprise; not in money as we so often think, but costly in human life. Often the alabaster cruse of life's precious ointment must needs be broken and poured out at the Master's feet! But let no man say, "Why this waste?"

Our Kurnool Home

When Fanny and I went out to India we expected to live in a mud hut. What was our surprise, as we climbed out of the old ox-cart that November morning, to find a substantial bungalow built of stone and set in a lovely garden of flowers and tropical plants. We discovered then to our surprise that substantial houses in India are built either of brick or stone for the simple reason that wood is not available, except expensive teak wood which is used only for roof-beams and for doors and windows. India is a hot country. Some one has said that for six months it is hot and for the other six months it is *hotter*. When we went out to India in our first term of service, we kept a thermometer on the back veranda of the bungalow. It was a bit exciting to watch the mercury rise higher and higher—105, 110, 115 degrees in the shade—and the longer I watched the hotter I got. So finally I smashed the thermometer and we have been cool ever since. However that may be, in a country such as India houses must be constructed to withstand the heat as far as possible. Verandas must be wide and deep. Walls must be thick and ceilings high. A second story has been found essential to provide sleeping quarters well above the ground. In the early days of the mission we had no protection against mosquitoes which in the monsoon and cool seasons make life almost unbearable. Fortunately one of our mission secretaries visited us in the height of the season and after being well bitten by these vicious little fellows, he at once recommended that all mission bungalows be screened. Thanks to his "bites" we now enjoy that protection.

The missionary in India, it must ever be remembered, lives in a hot and debilitating climate. The sun is a deadly enemy to the white man (let him not go out of doors without his *topee)*, small-pox and cholera and typhoid fever are epidemic three months in the year, disease lurks in every drop of water and the deadly *cobra* slips into your bathroom and coils himself in a corner ready to strike the venomous blow that means instant death. The utmost precaution, therefore must be taken to guard and preserve the health of the missionary that he may be kept "fit," able to bear the heavy burdens which rest upon him and to render the utmost service to the needy and suffering people among whom he labours in love.

After the Thomssens left for America, Fanny and I took possession of the bungalow. Here was to be our home and here we were to dwell for many a day in a strange land and among a strange people. Fanny was a real home-maker and she addressed herself to the new task with enthusiasm and delight. We had brought from America many lovely things, gifts of our parents and dear friends in the homeland. What a time we had fixing up the old bungalow! When it was finished, she proudly showed me all that she had done and I said, *"You have made a home in the wilderness!"* Many times, long afterwards, in the stress and strain of our busy life, while touring afar off along the hot and dusty roads of old Kurnool and over the sun-baked plains, the thought would come to me of that lovely home she made in the wilds of India and of the sweet and gentle wife whose hand and heart had fashioned it, and I thanked God for her. From that home seemed to come a fragrance, a breath of heaven!

Our Garden

Fanny loved flowers and all through the years of our life in India she had our house filled with them. So we got busy about a garden. This was something of a problem, for the soil in the mission compound was poor in quality and only about a foot in depth, being underlaid with a substratum of rock. It was necessary, therefore, to dig deep pits for the trees and shrubs by blasting out the rock and filling in with silt from the river-bed. This we did and in course of time and with no little sweat of the brow, the barren and rocky compound was converted into a beautiful garden. All kinds of tropical trees and shrubs were planted—the flowering rain tree, the royal poinciana,, (flame of the forest) with its masses of bright red flowers, the giant banyan, with its hundred-pillared roots and wide-spreading branches, the stately royal palm and the betel nut, the yellow bamboo and the almond tree. Rows of hibuscus in red, yellow and pink bordered either side of the roadway; oleanders covered the compound walls with masses of red, white and pink flowers. And there were marvellous crotons with leaves spotted, variagated and curled, and gorgeous red and white lilies.

To the rear of the bungalow we made our fruit garden. From Bangalore we brought the *Belgaum* orange. Having been brought up in Florida in the midst of marvellous orange groves, I firmly believed that the Florida orange was the finest in the world. But after tasting the Belgaum orange I had to admit that the Florida orange was not in it. The Belgaum is a loose-jacket orange, sweet and juicy, almost red in color and divided into well-defined quarters. Having tasted a Belgaum orange, you will never want any other. We purchased grafted trees on native stock, three years old, and within two years were bearing.

From Banganapalle in the Kurnool district, famous for its mangoes, we brought a collection of the choicest graft mangoes—the *Raspuri,* with its lovely green and red cheeks, the *Neelam* which bears twice in the year, the *Mulgova,* the largest and most luscious of mangoes and many other choice varieties. The mango is the most delicious of all Indian fruits. It must be tasted to be appreciated. If I were to attempt to describe it, I might say that it is a combination of our peach, pear and banana—rich and luscious. You cut it in half and eat it with a spoon and so juicy is it that in India they say you must eat your mango over the bathtub. The mango tree blooms in January and the mangoes ripen in May and June, the hot season in India.

From Bangalore we brought the *papayya*. The papayya tree looks much like the palm. It has a straight smooth trunk with branches at the top and clusters of fruit at the base of the branches. The fruit of the common varieties is of inferior quality, somewhat bitter and filled with seeds. But the graft papayya of the "melon" variety is very fine. As its name indicates, it is like a melon in shape, about nine inches in length, seedless, with reddish yellow meat and delicious to taste. In our Kurnool garden we planted a grove of twelve or fifteen of these fine papayya trees. They were loaded with fruit and we were very proud of them. Beside the oranges, mangoes and papayyas, we had pumaloes, which are somewhat like our pink grapefruit, only much larger. We also had guavas, pomagranites, and Bullock's Heart and Custard Apples, the sweetest of all fruits.

What, then, does all this have to do with missions, you ask? Much, every way. After a gruelling day in the heat and stench of a *Madiga palem,* after a grinding tour of a month or six weeks under a blazing tropical sun in the dusty, crowded villages of India, it was good to come home and walk in the garden in the "cool of the day" and drink in the fragrance of the flowers and refresh one's self in the beauty and the glory of God's creation. That little garden, to the weary traveller, looked very much like the Garden of Eden! So to His servant cometh strength for the morrow.

IV

LAYING THE FOUNDATIONS

After two months of happy fellowship with the Thomssens and a never-to-be-forgotten tour down the Kurnool-Cuddapah Canal, on January 15, 1895, we took over charge of the work, bidding the Thomassens *bon voyage* as they turned their faces toward the homeland. We were young and inexperienced with only two years of service in India and with a very limited command of the Telugu language, but we had the buoyancy of youth and the enthusiasm of the young missionary. The years immediately following were critical and momentous, for in that period the foundations were lead on which the structure of the coming years was built.

First Contacts

In our first year on the Kurnool field we had the unspeakable joy of preaching the Gospel to the Telugus for the first time. Two memorable tours were made—one in the eastern and the other in the western portions of the field. Taking our band of preachers along with us and pitching our tent in important centers, we preached the "Good News" in every village within a radius of five miles on either side of our route. We were surprised and gladdened beyond measure at the reception given to the Gospel message. In one village a *Sudra* (caste person) of the weaver caste heard the Gospel, came and wept over his sins and confessed his belief in Christ. Another *Sudra* declared that he and many others like him were ready to leave their religion and be baptized, if only they might receive the Lord's Supper *separately*. So early in our missionary life we realized the deadly power of *caste* in this land.

Ofttimes, however, the word found immediate lodgment. One Sunday morning as we entered the little chapel at Atmakur where our people were assembled for worship, we were astonished to see a Hindu *sannyasi* in his yellow robes with long matted hair and ashes smeared over his forehead and arms, seated in the audience among our people. As I preached from the text, "Behold, I stand at the door and knock; if any man will open the door I will come in," he seemed deeply moved. After the service he came to my tent and said, *"Sir, I will follow you."* I was astonished. On questioning him closely, he seemed quite determined and ready to forsake all for Christ. Without hesitation he joined us on tour. Very soon I found, as is so often the case with these so-called "holy men", that he was addicted to the use of *banghi* (opium). I told him that if he would follow Christ, he must give up the drug. At once he threw it away and from that day never touched it again, declaring that even the craving for it had vanished. The *sannyasi* had a little musical instrument, made of a gourd with a one-string attachment, used by Hindu holy men as they sing their *bajanas* (songs). As we went from village to village preaching in the bazaars, he would take his place beside the preachers, playing his *ekanatham* (instrument), singing our Christian songs and bearing his testimony to the saving power of Christ. In the course of our tour we came to his village where some of his relatives lived. We warned him that they might cast him out or even do him some harm, because he had broken with his ancestral religion. One night he disappeared and we could find no trace of him. What happened to him we never knew but we felt sure that his people, as so often happens in such cases, had put an end to him. We grieved much for our *sannyasi.* How difficult for a caste man to enter the Kingdom! It is easier for a camel to go through the eye of a needle! But with God "all things are possible."

The following year, on tour in April, we had a joyous time preaching the Gospel. We visited Banganapalle, a little Mohammedan state, fifty miles from Kurnool, where the Gospel had scarcely ever been preached. Everywhere we found open doors. In our report that year we said: "Personally the year has been one of great profit and blessing. We have learnt many things. Our experience in preaching to the Hindus has been a most blessed one, teaching us that the only thing about our religion that is really *new* to the Hindu is the story of the *Cross.* That alone has power to stir his heart to repentance." May we add that this remark is just as true today as it was fifty years ago!

The overshadowing event of the year 1897 was the *famine.* In every way within our power we gave ourselves to relieving the distress of the suffering people. We worked very largely in cooperation with the government as a member of the Indian Famine Charitable Relief Fund, distributing famine relief, giving grain doles to the aged and the destitute, opening kitchens for mothers unable to work and for orphan children, and when the rains came, distributing seed grain to poor farmers that they might sow their fields. All this brought us into intimate touch with the people and was an experience which we shall never forget. After the shadow of famine lifted and the fields were green once more with the springing crops, there was a great turning of the hearts of the people to the Lord. Twelve new villages came over to Christianity and ere the end of the year one hundred and thirty-seven persons were received by baptism. With a joyful note we closed the year: "Out of darkness God has brought light. He has turned our sighing into joy. The year has been abundantly fruitful. We have seen the Kingdom of

God come with power."

In 1899 we had the joy of baptizing one hundred and seventy-six persons, the largest ingathering in any one year of our service. These baptisms were from twenty-three villages, in widely separated parts of the field, nine of them receiving the Gospel for the first time. In our report of that year we said:

> Christianity is spreading from village to village. Wherever we go there is responsiveness to the Gospel call. Whole **palems** come to us, bringing their idols and charms and **deva** pots to be broken up or burnt. The Spirit of God is moving mightily upon the hearts of the people.

When we returned to the United States in 1900 after eight years in the country, the church membership on the Kurnool field had risen to over nine hundred, nearly doubling in our first term of service.

Teaching and Training

One of the first things we did after coming to Kurnool was to visit the Christians in the villages. We were more interested in them than in anything else. As we saw the condition of many of them we were saddened beyond expression. This experience with the Christians convinced me of the necessity not only of developing a strong and intelligent Christian community, but of raising up a force of educated and trained Indian workers to be the leaders of the people. This called for boarding schools, where the brightest boys and girls from the villages could be gathered and trained as Christian workers. When we came to Kurnool the Thomssens had already opened a little boarding school with twenty-four boys from one of the villages. This was a good start and we speedily increased the number to forty. In our first report on the Kurnool field we stressed this new undertaking:

With the great dearth of workers on the field, these schoolboys are the light of our eyes and the hope of the future. We are working for the spiritual development of every boy with the deepest solicitude and praying that the Holy Spirit may separate from among them chosen vessels to bear His name to the people sitting in darkness and the shadow of death.

Feeling the need of trained women, also, in the development of the work, we opened a girls' boarding school in the compound. We had no building and no funds, but we laid the foundations in faith and God wonderfully supplied our need. The following year the first girl from the outcaste *Madigas* on the Kurnool field passed her primary examination! The work rapidly progressed. The boys' school was raised to the lower secondary grade with a class of eleven boys in the first form. Feeling the need of closer contact with these young lives and deeper spiritual instruction, we cut out our vacation to the Hills and during the hot season in May with the thermometer at 110 degrees in the shade, we held a Bible class with the fourth and fifth standard boys, taking the Parables of Jesus for our study. A wonderful time we had with these boys that summer! We were on the mountain-top without going to the Nilgiri Hills! Long years afterwards they would speak of those days in the little chapel, when the Word of God was opened to them and their hearts burned within them as the Master spake unto them!

Year by year we continued to raise the grade of the boys' boarding school to meet the requirements of the field. Finally in 1898 we secured the services of an exceptionally capable head master of fifteen years' experience as a teacher in a mission high school and opened the third form, thus establishing a complete lower secondary school. Hindu boys flocked to our school in large numbers, many leaving the municipal high school to come to us. Having over a hundred Hindu boys under our instruction, we took every possible means to sow the good seed of the Kingdom in their young hearts. Under the capable management of our head master the school attained a high degree of efficiency and in 1899 fifteen boys were sent up for the government lower secondary examination, of whom nine passed. Of the three Christian boys sent up, one passed—*the first Christian boy to pass the lower secondary examination in the Kurnool mission!* The outcaste Madiga, once so despised and degraded, by the grace of God had begun his upward climb to Christian manhood!

One of the most important events of the year and one that gave us unfeigned joy was the sending forth of five of our boarding school boys into the work as village teachers. This was not our original plan. We had thought of giving the boys all the education they could take. But the call for workers was so persistent and imperative and the dearth so great, that we were forced to look to our boys as the only source of supply. At first we thought of sending out only one of them, but as soon as the matter was agitated four others volunteered. After much prayer we felt it was of the Lord and commending them unto Him we sent them forth. The following year eight more boys were sent forth, making thirteen in all. Through these boys our village schools experienced a remarkable development, the number of schools and pupils more than doubling in two years. In our report for the year we said:

> Wherever these boys have gone new centers have opened, converts have been gathered in and Christianity has taken a new hold. We are sending the boys out as fast as they are ready. The calls are more than we can meet. There are a half-dozen villages waiting today with pledges of money for preachers and teachers. This accession to our ranks has aroused a spirit of enthusiasm in all our workers. There is a harmony and spirit of brotherly love, a unity of purpose and devotion to the work such as we have never seen before.

Thus was fulfilled long-cherished hopes and plans for the

raising up of a force of trained and educated Indian Christian workers on this needy field.

Birth of a Church

When we took over the work of the Kurnool field, Atmakur was the only church on the field, with the exception of the station church. Realizing the importance of the Christian church in the growth and development of a strong and vigorous Christian community, we took steps at once to develop church life. Our preachers were stationed at important centers where there was the possibility and promise of growth into organized churches and were given charge of a group of villages about this center. It was not long before this policy began to bear fruit. In our report of 1897 perhaps the most significant paragraph is the following:

> One of the most encouraging events in the past year has been the birth of a new church on the Kurnool field. For over a year the Christians at this center have been a great joy to us. They have steadily grown in faith and zeal and love and we have long felt that the time had come for them to enter into the full privileges of church life. The Lord led us into the realization of our hopes and desires for them even sooner than we had expected. On November 14, 1895, the Gudur Baptist Church was duly organized with a membership of sixty in three different villages. They chose their own pastor and deacons and hereafter will observe the ordinances and conduct their own affairs as a regular church. We are happy to report that they at once assumed the entire support of their pastor.

This was the first step in the organization and development of independent churches on the Kurnool field. Gudur is a large and important village, twenty miles west of Kurnool, situated in a rich and populous region with great possibilities of growth and development. The church at this center entered upon its new life under the happiest auspices.

In our very first year on the Kurnool field the matter of *Christian giving* was strongly urged upon our people. As a result the Kurnool church chose an evangelist to preach the Gospel in the unevangelized regions of the field and assumed his entire support. Every Christian on the field pledged some amount, however small, to the service of the Lord. This continued for a year with encouraging results. Then the famine of 1897 which I have already described came and all our hopes were dashed to the ground. But in that very year and, indeed, as an outcome of the famine, a most remarkable movement sprang up among our Christians. I cannot do better than to describe this in the words of my report of 1897:

The most significant event of the year has been the movement toward self-support that has taken place on our field in the past few months. We speak of it as a "movement", for it has not been local, but wide-spread embracing the whole field. It has been a movement among our Christians to give a tenth of their substance to the Lord. It began among the Christians themselves, without any suggestion from the missionary or from any outsider, and, strange to say, it sprang out of the famine. In Gudur village, when the first rains came after the famine, the Christians promised, as they sowed their seed, to give one tenth of the crop to the Lord. The result was that at the harvest time on the Sunday when they brought their offerings to the house of God, they gave enough to support their pastor for six months! This was a revelation to me and opened my eyes to the possibility of Christian giving on the part of our people. We took up the work at once and went over the whole field, presenting to our Christians the teaching of God's word on the tithe. We have been astonished and over-joyed at the response. Every Christian has pledged some proportion of his income to the Lord. The amount has varied from a tenth to a sixtieth. It is yet too early to report much as to results. But this much may be said. Wherever we took the word of God and presented the matter with the help of the Holy Spirit there was deep searching of heart and the pledges were made with joyous freedom. This movement has taken deep hold both of the Christians and of the preachers and we believe it is of God.

The most important thing to note in this report is that self-support was not made the objective; in fact it was scarcely mentioned. We simply pressed home upon the hearts of our Christians their duty to give to the Lord of that which He had given to them. We found this appeal to work most powerfully and pledges were made by the whole body of our Christians.

The following year during the months of March and April in the harvest time, we went from village to village and had a glorious ingathering. Very little money was given. Almost all was in kind. Baskets and bags of grain, sheep, goats, chickens, eggs, vegetables (in one case, a *cow*) were brought to the house of God and offered with prayer and praise to Him who had given the harvest. The grain was not given to the preacher, but sold and the money deposited in the church treasury. On this tour a grand total of Rs 123 was collected. After all the offerings were made and it became known how much the Christians of a certain village or group of villages had given and the amount expected during the year, we asked them to decide how much they would give monthly towards the support of their preacher. The Atmakur church voted to take the whole support of their pastor. In other cases one, two or three rupees were pledged. In every case some proportion of the preacher's salary was assumed by the Christians.

One difficulty, however, arose. During the hot months, when there is no work for the poor people and when existance itself is a fierce struggle, we saw there was danger of their pledges lapsing. So we gave a pot to each family that would agree to put into it daily a handful of grain for the Lord. This was to be done by the women when they prepared the daily meal. We called this the *"Lord's Pot"* and had it labeled with the woman's name and a verse of Scripture. These handfuls of grain yielded, in some cases, as much as a rupee and a half or two rupees per mensem.

In this way, by the giving of the tithe and the grain in the pots we collected from our Christians during the year the sum of Rs 402; and the following year (1899) the contributions rose to Rs 453. When you remember that these poor people had never given anything before, the result is astonishing. Through these gifts of the people every preacher and teacher received some portion of his salary from the people to whom he ministered.

Ministering to the Poor and Needy

One of the by-products, so to speak, of this giving to the Lord was the revelation of the deep poverty of the people. When they began to bring in their little baskets of grain and we realized that this was the tenth of their harvest for the whole year, we had a concrete and vivid picture of their economic condition. They had always called themselves poor, but now we knew that they *were* poor. This led us to raise the question of doing something to lift them up, to some degree at least, and make them independent. As we began to study the problem, we found that large tracts of government waste lands were available and could be had for the asking. We became convinced that if the Christians could be put in possession of land, no better form of self-help could be devised. It would sweep away many of the disabilities which were dragging them down, not only materially and socially but spiritually as well. It would inspire them with new life and hope and at the same time make possible the attainment of self-supporting churches. Accordingly we petitioned the government and after much effort and many delays we finally secured lands for nearly all of our people. The amount per capita was small (an average of about three acres per family) but the value to the poor landless outcaste was inestimable.

With our own hands we measured and divided the lands into plots according to the number of families. When the work in each village was completed all were called together and, kneeling down in the open field under the bright sky, prayer was offered to God, the giver of every good gift. Lots were then drawn, each one receiving the portion which fell to him. When the last lot was assigned and every family had taken possession, there was much rejoicing. All felt that the land was the gift of God to be used for His glory. A new incentive was given to them to dig out of the soil an honest and well-earned livelihood.

Touring the villages, preaching the good news of the Kingdom, teaching the lowly and the outcaste the things of God, planting the Christian church in Indian soil, developing self-support, ministering to the poor and needy—this was our work in those early days and on this foundation we built for the coming years.

V

HOME LIFE IN INDIA

In the fall of 1900 after eight years of happy and fruitful labour in India, we returned to America on furlough. There, in Fanny's old home where we were married and from whence we sailed for India, two of our children were born—Edwin (our Ed as we love to call him) on February 22, 1901, and Katharine, on September 9, 1902. After crossing the seas ten thousand miles and living for eight years in the jungles of India, it seemed wonderful that two of our children should be born in the old Bouckville home! Surely an unseen Hand guides our steps!

In the spring of 1902 I was called to Hamilton, my old college town, to teach missions in the theological seminary for the spring semester—a call which brought me in contact with a fine group of young men studying for the ministry and which proved a rich and rewarding experience.

After the birth of our little Katharine it did not seem advisable for Fanny to cross the ocean in mid-winter with two little children. So in January, 1903, I went out to India alone. This separation of the family, however, proved to be too trying and finally I decided, on my own responsibility and at my own expense, to return to America and bring the family out. Accordingly I cabled Fanny: *"Coming."*

On receipt of the cable message she was overjoyed and at once began to make preparations for the journey. In August I sailed for America, travelling third class from Colombo to Naples and by steerage from Naples to New York. Arriving in New York, after giving the the steward a tip of a quarter,

I had just five cents in my pocket! I went at once to Soph's home in Brooklyn (my sister-in-law) and there found a letter of greeting from Fanny in Bouckville with a five dollar bill enclosed—the exact fare to my destination!

I expected to take the family back to India at once, but hardly had I arrived in America when our Betty was attacked with measles which soon spread to the other children and finally I myself became a victim. Owing to this epidemic in our little family, our sailing for India was delayed until January, 1904. After this never-to-be-forgotten experience in the homeland and a thrilling voyage across the Atlantic in mid-winter, in February, with hearts full and overflowing with gratitude to God for His manifold mercies, we arrived in our old home in Kurnool ready and eager for the new tasks.

After an absence of three years it was good to be back in dear old Kurnool once more. Our little family had now grown to number five. Beside Mum and Dad were the three children—Betty a beautiful girl of ten, with golden locks and rosy cheeks, Ed, a sturdy little follow of three, and Kathy, the sweet babe of eighteen months. It was a jolly home with the bright faces and the loving laughter of little children. The Hindus love the home and little children, and our Christian home made a powerful appeal to them. It spoke a language they could understand. It touched their hearts and opened the door of friendliness and good will. Every child was a little missionary.

Many happy times we had with our children—birthday parties out under the great banyan tree, trips in the house-boat on the Kurnool-Cuddapa Canal, camping at Sunkesala on the banks of the Tungabadhra River (with the roar of the water over the anicut lulling one to sleep) swimming, fishing, hunting ducks in the river bed. All these thrilling experiences made the home life a delight.

Three little Indians—Betty, Ed and Kathy—in Indian costume.

Soon the time came for the children to go to the schools for European children on the Nilgiri Hills, seven thousand feet above the sea, where the climate was cool and bracing and the flowers were always blooming. Betty and Kathy went to Hebron, Coonoor, and Ed to Breeks Memorial at Ooty. The holidays came in December, so that the children could be at home at Christmas. The home-coming was a wonderful time—the ride down the ghaut, the meeting with Dad at Guntikal with the big tiffin-basket, and finally the joyous meeting with Mother in the dear old home. How wonderful all the familiar sights and sounds—the salaams of the Telugu boys and girls in the compound, the greeting of old Papiah, the gardner, Ayanna, the bandy-man, and Venketiah, the cook; the Christmas tree in the home with Dad as Santa Claus; the presents bound with gay ribbons; the *bellum* and *pappalu* (sweets) for the servants and at night the big *bojanam* (feast) of rice and curry out on the tennis-court, with the boarding school boys and girls and the compound people! Wonderful days were these and wonderful times! In all these activities Fanny was ever the loving Mother, watching over her children and her family with unwearied devotion and presiding over the home with grace and charm.

Fanny's activities were by no means confined to the home. She was musical and loved her music. Endowed with a rich contralto voice, a graduate of the New England Conservatory of Music, she went out to India with high hopes of making much of her music. At the beginning of our missionary life, however, she had a rude shock. On our arrival at Bapatla, our mission station, we were given a grand welcome by the Indian Christians, garlanded with flowers, sprinkled with rose water, presented with betel-nut and a lime, in true Indian style. Among the items in the program was a song by a professional Hindu singer. To the accompaniment of the Indian drum and cymbals, the Hindu artist, with many facial contortions, struck the high notes in the Telugu musical scale until Fanny's nerves were all on edge and she cried out, "Is this Indian music?" It was a disillusioned experience.

However, she did not give up. Many of the Telugu tunes had been reduced to musical notation and many English hymns translated into Telugu. We had a little Estey Organ and with that she led the singing in our church services, teaching the people to sing accurately and with expression. In the school entertainments, the Christian Endeavour Rallies and the English services she trained our young men and young women in their songs and recitations and plays, some of which were outstanding and highly artistic. The entertainment given to His Excellency Sir Arthur Lawley, Governor of Madras, on the opening of the Coles Memorial High School (in the presence of the Hindu and Mohammedan gentlemen of the town) was spectacular and won the highest praise from the Governor and all assembled.

Fanny also had the care and oversight of the girls in the Emilie Coles Memorial Girls' School in the compound, with nearly a hundred girls in the boarding. She had a little dispensary well stocked with quinine and Perry Davis Pain Killer and other simple remedies. Fevers, stomach-aches, itch and other common ailments were effectively treated and more serious cases were sent to the municipal hospital. A scorpion sting was about our worst fatality. The girls sleep on mats on the floor and often in the night one of these vicious little fellows would sting a girl. Then the girls would raise a terrible hullabalu and come rushing over to the bungalow with the suffering and well-nigh hysterical patient. One good remedy we had. However severe the case, Fanny would give the girl a dose of Perry Davis Pain Killer. This is a powerful medicine and when a good dose is taken it produces a burning sensation and relief is almost instant. We sometimes thought the effect was due more to the burning sensation than to any effacy of the medicine. Anyhow it did the trick and the girl went away happy!

Fanny also taught the girls to sew and make their own garments, to embroider and do drawn work and make lace. They became experts with the needle, making beautiful doillies, handkerchiefs, table-spreads and lace work in artistic designs. In recognition of her devoted service Dr. Coles ordered that the girls' dormatory should be called the FRANCIS STANTON HOME, with her name inscribed on a marble tablet set in the wall.

In many respects Fanny's most important work was with the women. We had a remarkable group of Christian women in Kurnool—the Pastor's wife, the head mistress of the Mohammedan Girls' high school, the head mistress of our caste girls' school, teachers in the municipal Hindu Girls' school and in our Emilie Coles girls' school and our Bible women. With one or two exceptions they were all our own girls, educated and trained in our schools. Though sprung from the outcastes by birth, they were educated and trained women one of them a graduate of the Madras University and several trained matriculates. They were fine representatives of the new womanhood in India.

Once a week they had their meetings at the church, which they attended with great fidelity. Fanny always attended and always had a special message for them. Once a month she had them all come up to the mission compound with their babies and little children for a social gathering out in the garden on the tennis court. Refreshments were served. They played games and had good times together. Fanny was one amongst them, entering into all their joys and sorrows. She did not preach to them, but she lived the Christ-life as she walked among them and they all loved her and called her "*Talli*" ("Mother").

VI

TESTING TIMES AND REVIVAL

INDIA is a land of famine and pestilence. Some of the saddest experiences in missionary life, as well as some of the richest blessings, gather about these terrible visitations. What famine means to India is vividly set forth in my report of 1904:

> The only cloud on the horizon is the impending famine. The rains have totally failed and there is no harvest. Grain is selling at famine prices. Work is not to be had. The poor people are in great distress and unless government opens famine relief works soon, their condition will be critical. These oft-recurring famines are awful visitations. And worst of all they disorganize all lines of mission work. Schools are broken up; congregations scattered; self-support rendered impossible. All thought and effort on the part of the people centers in the one great struggle to exist. Our only consolation is in the thought that God is over all. He has seen fit to send the famine and He will bring good out of the seeming evil. Already the people are turning their eyes to Him who sitteth in the heavens and who alone can save them. May we be wise to discern the signs of the times, to see the outstretched hand of God and to go forward as He leads, whether it be in the darkness or in the light.

Following hard on the famine, in 1906 the triple scourge of typhoid fever, smallpox and cholera swept over the field and took its relentless toll of human life. Clouds and darkness overshadowed us. Calamities came thick and fast. The hand of our God was heavy upon us and upon our people. First, an epidemic of typhoid fever broke out in the boarding schools and one of our choicest boys, a student in the high school, and one of our brightest girls in the third form were taken from us.

As soon as the epidemic subsided, I started out on tour, but after two weeks of touring, the tent broke down and we had to return to Kurnool. I had the feeling, however, that for some reason the Lord had blocked the way and it was not long before it was made clear. The very day after reaching Kurnool I was stricken with smallpox. At first the doctor diagnosed it as typhoid fever and treated it accordingly, but after about a week the marks of smallpox began to appear and there was no doubt as to the nature of the dread disease. As soon as I realized what I had I knew that it was not safe for Fanny and the children to remain in the bungalow. Through the kindness of Mr. McKenzie, the British local fund engineer, who generously offered us the use of his bungalow, Fanny and the children were provided with a safe and comfortable home during my illness.

The Kurnool district surgeon, an Indian officer, treated me and wired for an English nurse from Madras, but neither the doctor nor the nurse were of much use. Four of our Indian Christians, Vandanam and Prasangi, teachers in the boarding school, Papiah, the gardener and Ayanna, the bandy-man, were my real nurses. Through all the long days and nights as the dread disease ran its course they stood by my side without the least fear of contagion, watching over me as a mother watches over a child. Humanly speaking, I owe my life to those four faithful and devoted Indian Christians.

As the disease progressed, my eyes became affected and I could not bear the light. The room had to be darkened and as the shades gathered about me, I thought I was going to be blind. After a month the crisis passed, strength returned and I could bear the light. I vividly remember that moment. As I looked out for the first time on the green mango trees surrounding the house, I wept for joy. The world looked so beautiful. It seemed as if I had risen from the grave and all was new. God had taken me by the hand and lifted me up!

The strain on Fanny was so great that as soon as I was out of danger she collapsed and for weeks was in a most critical condition. To add to her suffering it was the month of May, in the height of the hot season, and the heat was terrific. It was something that the "oldest inhabitant" had never experienced. Even with *Kus-kus tatties* and wet *punkas* and sprinkled beds, it was impossible to keep cool. Oh, how anxiously we looked for the coming of the monsoon and for the refreshing breezes of the life-giving rains! At last the rains came, bringing relief to the sick one. And slowly and tenderly we nursed her back to health and strength.

Scarcely had we recovered from this long siege of illness when we were plunged into an epidemic of *cholera.* It broke out in the town and district and raged with great fatality. A little boy came in with his people to the monthly meeting and was attacked and died in the compound. Though the boarding school children had just come in from the summer vacation, we had to send them home at once and close the schools for fear of an epidemic. Through the kindness of the district surgeon we were able to send out cholera medicine to the stricken people in the villages and many lives were thus saved.

There is scarcely anything more to be dreaded by the Christian missionary than an epidemic of cholera. At such times the people become wild with fright and an almost irresistable impulse seizes our Christians to join with the heathen in their terrible orgies by which they hope to appease the wrath of their gods. This time, however, our Christians stood firm. Gathering every night and morning in their little chapels and schoolhouses for prayers, they looked trustingly to God for deliverance. One of the most remarkable things was that in many villages the heathen joined with our people in their prayers, saying that only our God could save them. When cholera broke out in one of the villages and the people fled in terror to the fields, a Sudra of the shepherd caste took refuge with his whole family in the Christian chapel, beseeching that he might be allowed to remain among God's people, where, he said, he and his little ones would be safe. During all those terrible days he remained there, attending all the services and joining in the prayers himself in the name of Jesus!

The Great Revival

At last, after many days, suddenly and unexpectedly like the "rushing of a mighty wind", like "fire from heaven", the REVIVAL came. No words of mine can add to the story as it was written down in the fierce white light of those memorable days:

> As we look back upon it now, we feel that the Lord was preparing us through these afflictions for His visitation, showing us our utter helplessness and His all-sufficiency. Schools had been broken up, the work disorganized and the missionary smitten down. It was an hour of discouragement, almost of despair. But in that hour of darkness God came and spoke and we beheld His glory with astonishment and exceeding great joy. Our blind eyes were opened to the vision of God and our deaf ears were unstopped to the mighty pleadings of His voice. The light of God shone anew into our hearts, revealing, as of old, the glory of God in the face of Jesus Christ.
>
> A common quarterly meeting was turned into a revival lasting two weeks. The spirit of God was present in mighty power. His sharp two-edged sword pierced hearts through and through and smote them as unto death. We beheld at last our beloved Telugu brethren, for whom we had so often yearned and agonized in prayer, weeping over their sins, bowed down under conviction—yes, under conviction.
>
> How it came no one could tell. Without any leader, it began in a great volume of prayer, rising higher, and higher, all the people praying aloud and crying to God for mercy. All day and far into the night it continued and day by day grew in intensity. Many fell on their faces on the ground, crying out to God for mercy. Many were

weeping and confessing their sins. Some were beating their breasts and crying to God. Some had visions and trances. Some seemed as "possessed." Strange things happened—things we had never expected to see among our beloved Telugus—a people smitten and bowed down under conviction—a mighty struggle of souls with the powers of darkness. And finally, as confession was made, the burden of their sins "rolled away," hearts were cleansed and purified and they were filled with joy unspeakable and full of glory. Those days we shall never forget as long as we live. Those scenes were scenes of a lifetime—days of the right hand of the Most High!

The revival was by no means confined to Kurnool. It swept over the Telugu Mission like fire. Burning, cleansing and quickening, transforming lives by the divine power, it was a mighty *spiritual upheaval* such as had never been seen before. Not all of our stations were affected, but by far the larger portion received the blessing. Reports of the revival came from all over the mission, bringing joy to our hearts and assuring us that God was working everywhere.

What, then, shall we say to this mighty spiritual upheaval among the Telugus? Many things about it seem strange and disturbing to us of the West–the "visions", the "tongues", the "possessions", etc. But these were mere incidents, springing from the great emotional strain under which the people found themselves. We must not be disturbed by these things. How did the revival come? What were its essential and fundamental characteristics? And what were the results? These are the things we would like to know.

How the Revival came

In every instance, so far as we know, the human means employed by God to bring the revival was united and persistent prayer–prayer not of the missionaries, but of the people, and prayer not for revival in general, but for a reviving in each life. With hearts burdened for their sins and with inexpressible longing for cleansing and for power with God, the people met together day after day and, like the disciples of old, "continued with one accord in prayer and supplication." In some cases it was a week, in some cases a month or two months and in some cases only a few days. But as the volume of prayer went up, minds and hearts were centered more and more on the great need, desires and longings grew more intense and the little band of praying souls was drawn closer and closer by the bond of one great desire. At last, in God's own time, the answer came and frail human hands, as it were, brought down heaven's blessing. In these meetings the whole atmosphere was surcharged with the power of God. Strangers came into the meetings to mock and ridicule, only to be smitten down and convicted. Men and women left the meetings unable longer to bear the oppresive weight and wandered hither and thither, only to be drawn back as by an invisible hand to the mercy seat. The power set in motion by the cry of these united hearts was invincible and all-conquering. In this revival God magnified the mighty instrument of prayer which he has placed in the hands of His people and demonstrated anew that we have only to ask to receive!

The Spirit's Convicting Power

The greatest revelation of the revival was that the Indian Christian can weep over his sins. We had thought this impossible. We had thought there was something in the constitution of the Telugu, the Marathi, the Bengali, that made him incapable of feeling his sins as we do. Missionaries have worked twenty and thirty years among these people and have baptized them by the thousands, but with very rare exceptions have never seen them weep over their sins. This is just the opposite of what we would expect of an Oriental people.

The Hindus are by nature emotional, imaginative, mystical and deeply religious. We would have expected that their conversion would be marked by a profound sense of sin and a mighty upheaval of the whole being. Every missionary has seen such cases. I can never forget the conversion of a priest who had long sought God. When he found Him in Christ, his heart was melted within him, tears of penitence streamed down his face, the vision of himself in his lost and helpless condition was given him and he literally cast himself at the feet of his Lord and Master. But oh, how rare are such cases! How our hearts have longed to see such manifestations of God's power! The people have come; they have given their testimony; they have accepted Christ as Saviour, sometimes nominally, but in most cases truly. But there has been no deep stirring of the heart, no calling of deep unto deep in the inmost soul. As we have seen these things, we have been straitened within ourselves and have cried unto God with an exceeding bitter cry. "Oh, that the plowshare of God might be thrust into the hearts of these people, tearing up the deep roots of sin and creating a broken and a contrite spirit!"

In His appointed time the High and Holy One heard our cry. Tears of penitence were flowing from multitudes of hearts in our beloved India. Strong men were bowed down to the ground and weak women wept bitterly as when some loved one is lost. Hearts of stone were broken and shattered by the mighty hammer of God's spirit. The thorn-crowned head of Him whom they had pierced they saw—the bleeding hands and feet, the riven side. In bitterness of soul they cried: "My sins, O Christ, have nailed Thee to the cross and driven Thee unto death." As we saw these agonizings of the spirit in the hearts of the people, we were satisfied, for now we knew that there is no heart so hard, no people so far from God, no race so benighted as to withstand the mighty working of

God's spirit in the hearts of men. "For who shall abide His coming and who shall stand when He appeareth."

The Unseen Leader

One of the most striking features of this revival was that there was no human leader. No man originated it and no man guided it. The empty pulpit bore silent but eloquent witness to the fact that an unseen Leader was present. We missionaries have gone to the services with carefully prepared sermons, but have never delivered them. We have tried to guide the meetings, to make suggestions, but our words have fallen unheeded. We have tried to close meetings that would not close, to advise and exhort, but in vain. Formerly the people listened to us, hung on every word, but now they seemed to be listening to Another. Only that which springs up out of the people *carries*. What it would be no one could tell one moment beforehand. Prayer, praise, testimony, confession, one after another, all together, hour after hour. Often several stood at one time waiting to speak, again all prayed aloud at the same time. These were some of the characteristic features of the meetings. All we could do was to sit quietly by and let the work go on. If our hearts were touched by the power that was working, our prayer or testimony was blessed. If we spoke any other word, there was a strange, queer ring to it, as when a discord in music is struck.

What does all this mean? It simply means that God was in the midst of His people in a very real and actual sense. It means that the Spirit who was so real a personage in the history of the early church, who led every movement, who inspired ever action, who now sent forth and now held back, who continually filled and guided and quickened His people, was again in their midst.

We do not know just what was the "gift of tongues" in the early church, and perhaps it is just as well that we do not, lest we try to imitate it, but we do feel that the revival brought to the Telugu church *a* gift of tongues. Every experienced missionary will know what I mean by the *weariness of words* among the people of this land. With a remarkable gift of language and self-expression, whether in prayer or in testimony, it is words, words, words. The prayers of the people from the little child to the grown-up man are composed for the most part of stock phrases and set expressions that have long since lost all life and power. We have sometimes thought that this endless flow of words was one of the greatest curses of the Indian church. How often have we longed that they might fall upon their knees and utter the simple prayer of the publican, or rise and confess their faith in the simple, heaven-born confession of Peter! Hence it is that to us who have laboured long among these people, one of the most blessed fruits of the revival was the gift of a *new tongue.* It can be truly said now that they spoke, not in the old manner, but as "the Spirit giveth them utterance." New words and thoughts, new ideas, new conceptions of sin and self and God—these welled up out of their hearts and fell from their lips like the refreshing dew from heaven. Whence did they come? Where were they heard? Who taught them? There can be but one answer. The Spirit of Truth who guides his people into all Truth and takes the things of Christ and reveals them, *He* taught them. Here are just a few of these prayers and testimonies: "Thou, O Lord, art walking upon our hearts." "All the days of my life have been days of death, this is the day of my birth." "Hitherto, O Christ, Thou hast followed after me, henceforth I will follow after Thee." What depth of theology in this: "Thou hast created me to save me."

And what wonderful insight into the Atonement is this: "If we are so weighed down by the burden of our sins, what must have been the burden on the heart of Jesus when He bore the sins of the world!" In the revival at Kurnool, as the meetings went on, we found the people all "meditating on the cross", as they expressed it. Everybody was talking about *"siluva dyanam, siluva dyanam"* "meditation on the cross". Truly the Spirit still speaks and reveals unto babes things hidden from the wise and prudent.

The New Life

And finally what were the fruits of the revival? The fruits of the revival were seen in the lives of the people. "I am like a rope-walker," quaintly said one, "walking the rope of the new life, oh so carefully, lest I slip and fall." "We are so careful about our words now," said another, "and if a bad word comes, we feel so sorry." Strange things were happening. Men paid back money stolen or misappropriated, cleared off their debts, gave up tobacco and smoking. Women and girls brought their jewels and laid them on the alter of God. Quarrels were settled and enemies reconciled. Our schooboys, when they committed a fault, came running to us asking forgiveness. The daily round of work was done with a new spirit and there was joy even in the common tasks. Conscience was active and sensitive and the heart soft and tender. If wrong was done, penitence and contrition followed and forgiveness was sought at once. The revival brought these blessed fruits of the New Life–*the Life in Christ.* "Old things passed away; all things became new." We thank God for the great revival.

VII

COLES MEMORIAL HIGH SCHOOL: WINNING INDIA'S YOUTH

EDUCATION in Kurnool had its beginnings more than forty years ago in a little school of outcaste Christian boys gathered from one of the villages on the Kurnool field. The school rapidly grew from primary to lower secondary grade. An experienced head master was secured who brought the school to a high degree of efficiency. Hindu boys flocked to the school in large numbers, may leaving the municipal high school to come to us. In 1899 fifteen boys were sent up for the government lower secondary examination and nine passed-one of them the first Christian boy in the Kurnool Mission to pass the examination. With stations at Cumbum, Markapur, Nandyal and Kurnool in the Kurnool district, and Gadval, Palmur and Secunderabad in the Nizam's dominions, with a Christian community of some 18,000 and with over one hundred Hindu and Mohammedan boys under our care, we felt the time had come to open a high school. Furthermore, just at this time the leading Hindu and Mohammedan gentlemen of the town united in petitioning us to open a mission high school in Kurnool.

In due course the matter was laid before the Reference Committee of our mission and the opening of a high school was recommended. Accordingly on January 5, 1905, the American Baptist Mission High School at Kurnool was very modestly and unobtrusively opened. We had no great building to dedicate, no imposing structure to lend dignity to the occasion. The only available space we had was in the Book Depot, converted into a class-room for the newly opened fourth form, and there the work was begun. We had not even received the formal sanction of our Board, but we went forward in faith, believing it would come. We were not disappointed, for on April 22 the following letter was received:

> This will notify you that at the meeting of the Executive Committee held March 27, 1905, the following action was taken:
> VOTED: that on recommendation of the South India Reference Committee authorization is given for the establishment of a high school for boys at Kurnool.

That was a day of great rejoicing in Kurnool. Our prayer had been answered and our high school was an established fact. We were fortunate in securing the services of Mr. N. Narasayya, B.A.,L.T. as head master of the school. The total strength of the high school, including the lower secondary department was 183, of whom 36 were Christians, representing five mission stations. The Christian boys proved to be leaders in Christian Endeavor and in every good work and were most deligent and faithful in their studies. In our report for that year we said: "We are thankful for our high school and feel more convinced than ever that it is destined to be a mighty power for good throughout this whole section of the mission."

Government Recognition Refused

In the midst of our rejoicing, however, we met an unexpected obstacle in the Educational Department. In accordance with the rules of the Department we had made formal application to the Director of Public Instruction for recognition of the high school, since without recognition the school could not have government supervision nor could the pupils of the school appear for government examinations. Such recognition therefore was essential to the very existence of the school.

Just at the close of the year, however, while we were at Conference, word came from the Director refusing recognition. This extraordinary action was taken, not on the ground that our high school was not efficient or failed to meet government requirements, but simply on the ground that there was not room for two high schools in the town and the evident fear that if the mission high school were recognized the municipal school would go to the wall.

This was a stunning blow and seemed to be the shattering of all our fond hopes. However, convinced of the justice of our cause, we determined to fight to the finish and to use every means in our power to secure a reversal of the decision. Accordingly, through the Reference Committee of our mission we appealed to the Governor-in-Council, Madras. Fortunately, at that time, we had Lord Amptill as Governor of Madras—a broad-minded, Christian gentleman. Our appeal was laid before him, and, though he was on the eve of departure to England and pressed with the responsible duty of entertaining the Prince and Princess of Wales, he took time to consider our problem and passed in our favour, over-ruling the decision of the Director. This was a great triumph for our cause and for the cause of missions in general in India. In our report of that year we said: "We owe a great deal to Lord Amptill and we wish to express here our gratitude to him for his broad-minded and sympathetic action in this case. India is safe in the hands of such men." The Government Order of Recognition was received on February 21 and you may well imagine that there was great rejoicing in Kurnool. Three days later we held a public meeting to commemorate the event. It was largely attended by the leading Hindu and Mohammedan gentlemen of the town who had stood so loyally by us throughout the conflict. One of the leading lawyers of the town presided, the Government Order of

Top: Coles Memorial High School, erected 1908. Bottom: Statue of Dr. J. Ackerman Coles, M. D. L.L.D., erected by the Christians of Kurnool in commemoration of his munificent gifts.

Recognition was read and congratulatory speeches were made. Great enthusiasm prevailed.

A Great Gift

Shortly after this event, in the month of April, I was laid low with a virulent attack of smallpox. While lying in my darkened room, just after the crisis of the fever had passed, a telegram came. It was a cablegram from Boston announcing that Dr. J. Ackerman Coles and his sister, Miss Emilie Coles of New York, had given $10,000 for the high school building, to be called *"The Coles Memorial."* Tears of joy sprang to my eyes and I praised God for the wonderful answer to prayer. If I had had strength, I would have leaped out of bed and given three cheers. As speedily as possible the work of drawing up the plans and estimates were carried out and by November they were completed. On February 1, 1907, ground was broken for the building and on March 27 the foundation stone was laid by Dr. Downie, our veteran missionary of Nellore.

Opening of the COLES MEMORIAL

The year 1908 will always be remembered in the history of the Kurnool high school as the year of the opening of the new memorial building, the munificent gift of Dr. Coles and his sister, in memory of their father, Dr. Abraham Coles, and their mother, Caroline Ackerman Coles. On December 17 the building was opened by His Excellency Sir Arthur Lawley, Governor of Madras, with great eclat in the presence of a brilliant audience of the elite of Kurnool town and district. It was a great occasion, never to be forgotten in the history of the mission, the crowning event of the year and in fact of many years of labour and struggle. The following is my address delivered on the occasion:

TO HIS EXCELLENCY, SIR ARTHUR LAWLEY, G.C.I.E., K.C.M.G.
GOVERNOR OF FORT ST. GEORGE

May It Please Your Excellency: Compared with many of the old historic institutions which Your Excellency has honored with your presence and encouraged with your sympathy, the Coles Memorial High School is but an infant, but I trust it has shown even in its brief career, that it is withal a strong and sturdy infant, with promise for the future. It had its beginnings in a small school started sixteen years ago which grew from primary to lower secondary and later to high school grade. With a Christian community of over 18,000 and stations at Cumbum, Markapur, Nandyal, Gadval and the Nizam's dominions, a high school seemed to be urgently needed. This need was emphasized when a petition came from the Hindu and Mohammedan gentlemen of the town asking that such a school be established. In response to this urgent appeal and to meet the needs of our growing Christian community, this school was established in January, 1907, and was recognized by government the following month. The growth of the school demanded that a larger and more suitable building be provided. When I was home in America, I had the pleasure of meeting Dr. J. Ackerman Coles of New York, and his sister, Miss Emilie Coles, who generously provided the money—$10,000, or Rs. 30,000—for the building. On the twenty-seventh of March, 1907, the foundation stone was laid by Dr. Downie of Nellore. With this splendid accommodation and equipment and with an able staff of teachers and an American principal,who, we expect, will soon be sent out, we shall endeavour, as far as in us lies, to impart to the youth of this vicinity a sound education and to lay deep down in their hearts the foundation of a noble and exalted Christian character.

To this address His Excellency replied in part as follows:

"Mr. Stanton, Ladies and Gentlemen:

I have, as you are aware, wandered about the world in various directions and through various continents, and it has been my privilege to see, always with amazement and admiration, something of the work of America in distant lands. It has been my privilege to see something of the work of Dr. Downie and his noble fellow-workers in Nellore. I assure you that I esteem it a very great pleasure and a very great honour to have been able to formally open the Coles Memorial Building and to express my sense of admiration at the noble purpose and great generosity of him by whom this building was erected. What is the message this building brings to you and to me? Surely, if anything, it speaks of love, of self-devotion and self-sacrifice of the man who has given the best of his life to follow in the footsteps of the Master whom we serve. Surely this building, which owes its creation to the efforts of Mr. Stanton, is eloquent of human love, especially when we again think that its actual construction is due to the generous impulses and noble purposes of Dr. Coles and his sister. Shall not we all determine to follow, as far as we may, their example. To the boys of this school I would say, 'When you hear the bell let it remind you that love is the mainspring of life.' And, Sir, I would ask you to say to Dr. Coles and his sister that I, in my capacity as Governor of this great Presidency, desire to thank them most sincerely for the generous help which they are giving to the people of this land.

The message Sir Arthur Lawley delivered that afternoon, so sympathetic, broad-minded and large hearted, was a noble utterance, worthy of the man and the occasion. The building stood complete, a beautiful memorial, not unworthy, we trust, of the sainted dead in whose memory it was so lovingly erected.

The benefactions of Dr. and Miss Coles did not cease with the erection of the building. In addition to the gift of $10,000 they gave an additional sum of $1,900 for the equipment of the building on the most approved lines. This splendid gift was the more appreciated as our Board in Boston, on account of the financial stringency at home, were unable to provide the necessary funds for the equipment. Nor was this all. A silver-toned bell, specially cast in Troy, New York, for the Kurnool high school, two flags—the Stars and Stripes and the Union Jack, a complete set of the Encyclopedia Britannica and many other valuable historical and biographical works for the reference library were further tokens, if any were needed, of the deep and abiding interest of Dr. Coles in the great work he had inaugurated in India.

The work of the school during the year was carried on with renewed vigor and enthusiasm. The strength of the school rose from 196 in 1907 to 220 in 1908. Of these, forty were Christian boys, representing eight mission fields. Cumbum, Kanigiri, Markapur, Ramapatnam, Gadval, Donakonda, Nandyal and Kurnool. Had we the funds we could have doubled the number of Christian boys. We closed our report for the year with an urgent appeal for an American principal.

In an unexpected manner our prayer was answered. In the spring of 1910 we went home on furlough and while there, in 1911, Dr. Henry Huizinga, Ph.D. was appointed principal of the Coles Memorial High School. With an experience of more than twelve years in educational work in the Ongole college and high school, Dr. Huizinga came to Kurnool finely equipped for the new task. On our return to India in 1912 it was a great pleasure to find him in charge of the high school and to realize that at last a man had been found for this important work. However, after a short but strenuous term of three years during which a hostel for Hindu and Mohammedan students, a boarding home for Christian boys and a principal's bungalow were erected, he went home on furlough and Rev. B. J. Rockwood was appointed in his place. With the appointment of Mr. Rockwood, who served continuously in that capacity for 27 years until his retirement in 1942, the high school entered upon an unprecedented period of development, fulfilling our highest hopes and expectations.

Such is the story, briefly told, of the Coles Memorial High School from its inception as a little elementary school to its final growth and development into a strong and powerful institution of higher education. As we look back over the years of toil and struggle, it may not be amiss to ask ourselves what the high school stands for. What have been its aims and purposes and what has it achieved thus far in its history?

Training Workers

Our aim, first of all, in this high school has been to educate and train workers for Christian service. The first concern of every missionary must be the training of a band of efficient and spirit-filled native workers who shall carry the Gospel into every village and hamlet and make Christianity indigenous in the land. He must train up pastors for the churches, evangelists to preach the Gospel, teachers to instruct the youth, Bible women and Zenana workers to carry the Gospel into the homes of the people. It is not too much to say that our whole educational work, from the little pial village school to our finest high schools and colleges exist primarily to raise up such a body of native workers. This is not to say that we expect every Christian boy in our schools to become a preacher or teacher. But here is the source of supply. From among these boys we expect our workers to come and we do not know of any other way of procuring them. This is especially true of mission work in India where the great majority of our converts are from the outcaste classes—the lowest in the land. It is only in the rarest cases that a worker can be developed from among the adult converts of these classes. In our whole Telugu mission with a force of 1,500 native workers, I suppose there are not 20 men who have thus been trained. Practically this whole force is the product of our mission schools. Without such schools, therefore, to provide us with workers it would have been impossible to have gathered in and shephered our great host of 117,000 converts. The missions that are strong, vigorous and aggressive in India today are the missions provided with a complete educational system from the elementary grade to the collegiate in which a great host of Christian boys and girls are being trained for Christian service. The first and primary purpose of our educational work is to train such a body of native workers. This is what we have been doing in the Coles Memorial High School for more than forty years. I well remember the day away back in 1898, long before the high school was established, when, in response to the urgent call for workers, five of our boys in the boarding school, then only of lower secondary grade, volunteered to go into the work as village school teachers. With fervent prayer to the Lord of the harvest we sent them forth. The going out of these boys revolutionized our work. That process of training and sending out has been carried on through all these years. So that today all the pastors of our churches, both station and village, the field Evangelist, the station boarding superintendent, the head master of the Church school and his staff, many of the Christian teachers in the high school and the industrial school and all our village teachers—in fact practically all of the mission workers on the Kurnool field have been educated and trained in the Coles Memorial High School. Not only so, our Coles boys have gone out as mission workers to Cumbum, Markapur, Nandyal, Donakonda, Kanigiri and many stations in the Deccan. It is difficult, if not impossible, to estimate the significance and worth of a work so far-reaching as this.

Christian Leadership

In the second place, we have aimed in our high school not only to raise up mission workers, but to fit our Christian young men for leadership in their communities. It is evident that if Christianity is to become a permanent power in India, it must be maintained and propogated by something more than mission agents. With much labour and toil we have raised an army of mission preachers, pastors, evangelists, teachers and Bible woman, but we are saidly lacking in leaders among the rank and file of the Indian Christian community. We need leaders in the Christian community—men of strong and stalwart faith, of superior education and upright character, in every rank and profession of life, to be centers of life and power in the land, to mould and shape the society in which they live, to be forces for righteousness in the midst of the corruption about them and to draw their countrymen to Christ by the power of a noble and winsome personality. Such men—not agents of mission societies but laymen in the Christian church—living Christ in their daily life, and commending Him to all by word and deed, cannot fail to be powerful factors in the Christianization of India. They represent the ripened fruit of Christianity proving to Hindus that Christianity is not a foreign religion, but universal in character, striking its roots into Indian soil and bearing fruit under the Eastern sky as well as the Western. It is our duty then as "wise master builders" to train such leaders in the Christian Church. And where can we find them save among the youth in our schools? Such leaders as we have here described must surely have the best we can give them, the best of education and training, the best of Western culture and the best of Christian life and character. To produce such men we must begin with our boys in the early years, separating them from the blighting touch and the withering breath of heathenism, rearing them in a Christian atmosphere, moulding and fashioning, disciplining and teaching, exhorting in all long-suffering and patience, chastening in love and tenderly yet firmly leading them through years of training in boarding school, high school and college until at last we have produced a Christian man, ready to go out into the world and truly represent Christ to his countrymen. A difficult and arduous task is this and we must admit that we are far from realizing our ideal, but this is what we have been trying to do in Coles Memorial High School.

Christ and the Hindu Heart

Thus far we have been speaking of our educational work as related to the Christian community, but in our Coles Memorial High School we have always had a large number of Hindu and Mohammedan boys under our care and instruction, to be moulded and shaped for the Kingdom of God. What, then, has been our aim with reference to these boys? Our aim surely must be not merely to educate but to win these pupils to Christ. This must ever be the great objective of work among non-Christians. It is not enough merely to present the truth to our pupils, it must be carried home to the heart and laid upon the conscience. The religion we are commanded to teach is not a philosophy to be discussed but a truth to be accepted. It is personal and claimant. Until the insistant claims of Jesus as Lord and Master are felt and acknowledged by each one of our pupils, it cannot be said that we have delivered our message. Mission schools should be evangelizing agencies and we cannot expect them to be such until we make it our supreme aim to win our pupils to Christ. As we said in our address to the Governor on the occasion of the opening of the school, "We shall endeavour, as far as in us lies, not only to impart to the youth of this vacinity a sound education, but to lay deep down in their hearts the foundation of a noble and exalted Christian character."

How far, then, have these high aims been realized? The results of the work of higher education among non-Christians cannot be gauged by statistics or counted by the number of converts. Christianity is like leaven, hidden from view and working silently and mysteriously in the human heart and in society as a whole. We have been sowing the seed of the kingdom in class after class and we do not believe for an instant that it has been in vain. How much has sprung up and how far it has grown to maturity, it is impossible for us to tell. How many of these boys who have passed through our mission schools are secret disciples of the Lord Jesus, we cannot say, but we know that some are and we know that all such are known to Him whose they are. How much of superstition and darkness has been dispelled, how many barriers have been broken down, how many false ideas and un-Christian concepts have been eradicated and how much clearer and brighter the vision of the Crucified One has become to these young hearts, we cannot tell. We only know that this work is being done in the quiet of the classroom, before the open page of the Holy Book and under the life-giving breath of the Divine Spirit. And He will guard and keep it. But here too we do not feel that we have lived up to our responsibilities or adequately discharged our high duties. In a sense we plead guilty to the charge of failure in this work. We acknowledge that the results, both direct and indirect, should have been far greater. We confess that often we have been diverted from the main issue. In this educational work in particular we have often been "cumbered about many things" and that "better part" we have too often neglected. We have been trying to educate rather than Christianize.

The Claims of Christ

What, then, must we do? In the first place, we must press home the claims of Christ upon the hearts and consciences of our students. Our message is the "Good News" of Jesus Christ—a Divine message, incomparably greater than all the half-truths of Hinduism, self-evidencing in character, profound yet simple in substance, exalted in tone, heart-searching and will-compelling. This message we offer as worthy of all acceptation. Here are the quickening words of Life. Here lie enshrined the forces of a new faith. Here is a SAVIOUR, whom all the wisdom of the Vedas failed to discover—so beautiful, so holy, so tender, so "mighty to save!" *This Christ we offer.*

The Christian Teacher

In the second place, there must be *sympathetic contact.*

The greatest factor in the accomplishment of our purpose is the Christian teacher. The truth, however great, needs the living personality both to convey it and to illustrate it. It is a great thing to put the Bible into the hands of our pupils, but it is a greater thing to embody that truth in a life lived among them. Just as early Christianity was learnt not from the books, but from the living voice and the personal presence of Him who walked by the Sea of Galilee, so Christianity in India today is being learnt by the Hindus, not so much from the books as from the lives of the men who have caught the spirit of Jesus. There is much about the doctrine of Christianity to which the Hindu is not ready to subscribe, but the Christ-life and the Christ-ideal attract him and make a never-failing appeal. The men educated in our mission schools and colleges delight to tell of the Christian teachers at whose feet they sat and from whom they learnt so much of Christ. They may have forgotten all they ever learnt of the Bible, but they never can forget the men who taught them the Bible. It is the *man* after all, imperfect though he may be, who alone can interpret the Book and Him of whom it speaks. Such men in our schools and colleges today, filled with the love of Christ and dedicated to His service, have ever been and ever will be the mightiest factors in the Christianization of India. They are the true interpreters of Christ to the choicest spirits of the rising generation of India—channels of the Divine life and heralds of an everlasting Kingdom.

VIII

THE GREAT AWAKENING: THE UNTOUCHABLES BEGIN TO MOVE

AFTER a second term of seven happy years of service on the Kurnool field, in the spring of 1910, we went home on furlough. In Hamilton we spent a very delightful furlough, renewing the fellowships and associations of college days. We had planned to return to India in the fall of 1911 and, in fact, had our passage engaged for August 26, but Fanny was suddenly taken ill and we had to cancel the sailing. After a serious operation and many days of suffering, the Lord graciously raised her up and restored her to health and strength. The doctor said she might go back to India. Our prayers were answered.

The day before sailing was a sad one for us, for on that day we parted with our precious Betty. Oh, how it wrung our hearts! Fanny's grief was almost uncontrollable. I never realized before the depths of a mother's love. Betty was her first child. That day it seemed as if there had been a funeral in the house, it was so still and empty. This parting with precious children is the greatest sacrifice the missionary is called upon to make, but this also is for the dear Lord's sake.

On January 5 Fanny and I with our two little ones sailed from New York for Genoa on the old S.S. "Hamburg." Many loving messages from dear friends were received bidding us farewell. Dr. and Miss Coles sent a special letter wishing us a pleasant voyage and writing lovingly of our Betty. A beautiful letter was received from Dr. Clarke, my beloved teacher, and flowers from the Hamilton ladies. These loving messages brought sweet comfort and joy to our sad hearts.

In Perils of the Deep

On the voyage across the Atlantic, on the third day out, we encountered a terrific storm. Beginning about four o'clock in the afternoon, it continued all night. A great wave struck the ship on the port side and smashed in the double doors on the upper deck. A deluge of water poured down the staircase, sweeping away the steam radiator with a heavy marble top, tearing down the stair railing and sweeping on like a river down the corridors. Many cabins were flooded and the people forced to leave them. As quickly as possible the carpenters boarded up the doorway, but it took several hours to bail out the water. Very few passengers went to dinner that night and during the dinner hour one could hear the crashing of broken dishes with every lurch of the ship. There was little sleep for any of us that night. The ship rolled and pitched terribly. Our trunks played shuffle-board in our cabins and the noise of the storm was terrific. Finally the captain had to turn the ship about and head her into the storm to withstand its fury. Toward morning the storm abated a bit and we got a little sleep. All on board, both passengers and stewards, said it was the worst storm they had ever encountered. We all realized anew the greatness and power of God and our own helplessness. We were powerless to do anything. We could only be still and pray, for it seemed that at any moment the ship might go down. For five days the storm continued with only slight abatement. The ship was rolling and pitching and it was impossible to sleep at night. Finally we passed the Azores, where we found calm seas and were cheered by the sight of land.

Genoa, Naples, Colombo

On January 19 we arrived in Genoa, completing the first

stage of our long journey. At the Hotel Smith where we put up we met many delightful American people, among whom were Mr. and Mrs. Cortell of Boston—lovely people to whom we became deeply attached. But our joy was soon turned to sorrow, for on the third day after landing Fanny's old trouble started up afresh and greatly alarmed us. Poor girl, she was so exhausted and worn out with the long days of vigil and the sleepless nights, it was no wonder that she was almost in collapse. It was a time of intense anxiety. Here we were, scarcely started on our long journey to India! Visions of hospitals, doctors and operations came before me and almost drove me out of my mind. The way seemed dark and forbidding. Should we go on or should we turn back! We could not bear the thought of turning back. Nights were spent in prayer. God was very near. Our cry was to Him. Fanny was not able to lift her head from the pillow. After many weary days of anxious waiting, one morning I opened my Bible to Isaiah 41:13, "I, the Lord thy God will hold thy right hand. Fear not." How precious! How comforting! What harm could come nigh us! God the Almighty was holding our hand! Underneath were the "everlasting arms"! All fear fled away. God had heard our cry! That day was the turning point in Fanny's illness. Day by day she continued to improve and finally, with the doctor's consent, we engaged passage for India by the S.S. "Osterly", booked to sail from Naples on the twenty-fourth!

As though this were not enough, another very wonderful thing happened to us. Knowing the very heavy expense we had incurred by Fanny's serious illness and our enforced stay in Italy, our dear friends the Cortells offered to supply us with whatever money we might require. How wonderful that such friends should meet our need in a strange land! "My God shall supply all your need." On February 16 we left Genoa for Naples, where we were to take ship for India.

In my diary of that date is the following entry:

> February 16. Our last day in Genoa. Four weeks we have been held up in old Genoa as by an invisible Hand. How little we expected this when we came! How little we know what the morrow will bring forth! We shall never forget our experiences in Genoa. This place has been to us as the "house of God" and the "gate of heaven". Through suffering God has come very near, and we rejoice. We said goodbye to our dear friends, the Cortells, with deep regret. We shall always look upon them as angels to visit us in time of need.

We arrived in Naples the eighteenth. On the twenty-fourth we sailed from Naples on the S.S. "Osterly" of the Orient Line. As we sailed out of the beautiful Bay of Naples in the bright sunshine of a glorious Italian day, with our loved one restored to health and strength, bound for dear old India, it seemed like a dream. The glorious words of the Psalm came to our lips:

> Then was our mouth filled with laughter and our tongue with singing. The Lord hath done great things for us, whereof we are glad. They that sow in tears shall reap in joy. He that goeth forth weeping, bearing precious seed, shall doubtless come again with rejoicing, bringing his sheaves with him.

After a record voyage of only fourteen days from Naples, on March 9, 1912, we arrived in Colombo. When at last we planted our feet on India's soil and gazed once more on the old familiar scenes, we were overwhelmed with the thought that the Lord must surely have a work for us to do in India or we would never have reached these shores. Taking Fanny and the two little ones to the Hills, I went on to Kurnool, reaching the station on March 16. After a delightful welcome by Mr. and Mrs. G. J. Huizinga, who were in charge of the work during our absence, and all our beloved workers and Christians, we took up the reins once more and set ourselves to the tasks before us.

Revival in the Villages

In returning to India for the third time, we determined to give the primary place to evangelistic work, taking as our motto the words of the Apostle Paul, "For I determined not to know anything among you save Jesus Christ and Him crucified." The eighteen years we had spent on the Kurnool field had been years of testing for the young missionaries. Famine, cholera, smallpox and typhoid had swept over the field in frightful epidemics and we ourselves had not escaped, but through it all we had *held on* and God had not failed us, but rather had richly blessed us. The foundations of our future work had been well and strongly laid. Our churches had been placed on a self-supporting basis. The Coles Memorial High School had been established and had grown to be a strong and vigorous institution of higher education for India's youth. And, most significant of all, a great revival had swept over the field, transforming the life of workers and people. All this, by the grace of God, had been wrought. But no great ingathering among the heathen had as yet taken place and for this we longed and prayed. The revival of 1906 was almost exclusively confined to our Christians. In our report of that year, while rejoicing in the blessing poured out upon our workers and people, we said: "And now we are looking for the manifestation of God's power among the heathen. Shall this new year witness a mighty shaking of the dry bones of heathenism through the convincing witness of an awakened Church? This is our prayer." The new year did not bring that "manifestation". In fact, we had to wait *six* years before it came. We had to pass through "deep waters" and learn many things in the fiery furnace of afflication ere that "manifestation" came. But at last, after our return to India in 1912, the great awakening came.

I well remember that night. We were out in Polukallu, on the western confines of the Kurnool field, in the month of November, holding evangelistic meetings. The little chapel was crowded to the doors with some two hundred people, the men on one side, the women on the other and the children in between. As we preached to the people that night they seemed so eager to hear, so expectant, so seriously minded, that we felt moved to call upon them to take their stand for Christ. Strange to say, we had never done this before in our preaching in India. We had preached to the people and left the message with them and then moved on. But it seemed now as if the time had come for decision and that we could well call upon them to break with the past and come out on the Lord's side. So we gave the invitation. "If there are any here who want to follow Christ," I said, "let them stand up." Immediately a man arose and said: *"Ayya, nenu numminanu"* ("Sir, I believe.") And one after another five men rose and confessed their faith in Christ. There was no doubt about their seriousness and sincerity and all present were deeply moved. It was a great meeting and the Spirit of God was present in power. The next night the crowd was so large that there was not room inside and we met out in front of the chapel in the moonlight. Preacher Ramiah told the story of his conversion with great power. Then I called upon them to take their stand for Christ. Twelve men arose, one after another, and confessed Christ. It was an inspiring sight. God was in our midst. A great door seemed opened before us and we praised God for the manifestation of his power. After this blessed experience of God's quickening and reviving power in the hearts of the people, we went on with the gracious work, holding revival meetings in every village, both in the eastern and western portions of our field. Like Cornelius of old, everywhere the people were waiting and expectant. In some cases we had meetings with no apparent result and went

Top: On tour—old style. Ox cart going three miles an hour. Center: On tour—new style. Dr. and Mrs. Stanton in car given by the First Baptist Church, Hollywood, California. Bottom: Baptisms in the Kurnool-Cuddapa Canal, great in-gathering among the Outcastes.

back to our tent disheartened and discouraged, but after I had gone to bed the people came running to our tent asking to be baptized. In one village only one or two rose in the night meeting. The people seemed hard and unresponsive. But we found that after we had gone away they got together and discussed the great question far into the night and when we went to the *palem* in the morning, fourteen took their stand for Christ. Many new villages came over to Christianity. In one of these, Nandikotkur, a *taluq* town, we had worked for twenty years but could get no hold on the people. This time they sent messages to us to come to their village. At night the whole *palem* gathered together to hear the word of God. We had one of the most powerful meetings I have ever witnessed in India. Thirty families, men and women, took their stand for Christ. The whole *palem* was moved as by a common impulse.

In many of our old villages also, where we had had Christians for twenty or thirty years, the Lord wrought a not less remarkable work of grace. Though we had worked so many years in these centers, half of the *palem* was still heathen and the heathenism seemed denser and darker, if anything, than in untouched villages. To these people our religion had become an old story and they seemed as truly "gospel-hardened" as any such people in the homeland. After this gracious work of revival began, it was laid upon our hearts that now was the time to reach these needy souls. The first village of this kind we visited was Gadidamudagu, where there had been Christians for twenty years but half of the *palem* was still heathen and the old *Maramma* temple still stood. That night we left the chapel where we were accustomed to hold our meetings and went right down into the midst of the *palem* where the people lived. A great crowd gathered and the Spirit of God was present in power. When the opportunity was given them to take their stand for Christ, one after another arose, men and women, expressing their desire to become Christians, and when the meeting closed we found not a heathen was left in the *palem*. This was repeated in three other villages on the field.

In the last village visited on this tour, we had, perhaps, the most remarkable result. While we were preaching, a man stood up and said he was a *Mala* (one of the divisions of the outcastes) and wanted to become a Christian. We pointed out to him that none of his people had ever joined our mission and that he might be severely persecuted if he took this step. He insisted that he was quite prepared to endure all and if we would come to his *palem* in the morning, he would have all his people ready to hear our message. In the morning we went, and eight of the leading men took their stand for Christ. These were the first *Malas* who had ever joined our mission on the Kurnool field and our prayer went up to God that they might be the first fruits of a great harvest among this class.

The Outcastes turn to Christ

On this tour of one month and fifteen days, in November and December, over three hundred people in twenty villages took their stand for Christ. In our report of 1912, speaking of this great awakening, we said:

> It looks as if we were to have a great movement to Christianity among the outcaste peoples on this field. Certainly, in the eighteen years we have been working here, we have never seen any such awakening as this. The prophetic words of John the Baptist are continually ringing in our ears: "The time is fulfilled and the Kingdom of God is at hand." We believe it is—the Kingdom of God for the outcaste! And as the New Year dawns, our hearts are filled with an inexpressible joy as we look out upon the fields "white unto the harvest" and see the multitudes pressing into the Kingdom.

On this tour, as our time was limited and every hour was

taken up with the meetings, we did not baptize at all. We told the people to come to Kurnool at the first *nelasary* (monthly meeting) of the New Year on January 11 and we would baptize those who were ready. As this was harvest time and the busy season of the year, we were doubtful if any would come but we thought it would be at least a good test of their sincerity. But the movement was of God and nothing could stem the tide. Great crowds came from all over the field, some from villages forty, fifty and sixty miles distant. Sunday morning the little Rogers' Memorial Gospel Hall was packed to the doors. After the morning service we held a meeting to examine the candidates for baptism. It was a scene I shall never forget. Under the wide-spreading branches of the great banyan tree in the mission compound they gathered, an eager, restless throng, with a new light in their eyes and a new joy in their hearts. After the examination was over we took them down to the Tungabadhra River and, as the sun was setting over the Western hills, we led them down into the baptismal waters. That Sunday afternoon one hundred and thirty-two happy converts were buried with Christ in baptism in the waters of the old Tungabadhra River—the largest number ever baptized in a single day on the Kurnool field! It was a great day in the history of the Kurnool Mission!

This was the beginning of a movement which went on steadily during the year. At every *nelasary* great crowds of people came from the villages and our little chapel was packed to the doors. Taking the year as a whole, many of the old centers of work were revived and whole *palems* became Christians. Three hundred and sixty-two members were added by baptism to the church. Harvest-time had come.

During 1914 the movement continued to grow in depth and power. On a tour in the eastern portion of the field in the month of March, we found the Atmakur church greatly revived. The Christians had pledged themselves to witness for Christ wherever they went. Under this new impulse they visited a group of villages north of Atmakur. When I arrived on tour, they reported many believing in those parts. We were overjoyed to hear the good news. Here was the church really at work, carrying the Gospel far and wide. In response to urgent appeals from the people, we made a tour of the villages to the north. Everywhere we found the people eager to hear the word of God. In a night evangelistic meeting forty-six people took their stand for Christ. There was a great stirring among the dry bones of heathenism. On our return to Atmakur on the following Sunday, eager throngs of people came from the villages for baptism. It was an inspiring sight to see them trudging along over the dusty roads walking ten to fifteen miles in the hot and glaring sun. One could not but feel that there must be some deep desire in their hearts, impelling them to do this. That afternoon we had the joy of baptizing thirty-three happy converts in the old well in the tamarind tope at Atmakur. On this eastern tour we carried the Gospel into a new section of the field; four new villages were won for Christ and one hundred and eight people were baptized. In our report for 1914 we gave this testimony,

> The movement among the outcastes which began on this field two years ago has continued during the year, gaining in intensity and strength. The number of baptisms, two hundred and seventy-eight, was not quite as large as in the previous year, but it was simply due to the fact that touring was greatly interfered with and it was not possible to get out on the field and gather in the converts. At our last nelasary the reports from the field showed that over two hundred people were waiting for baptism. The people are eager and expectant. On every side are open doors. In the past two years, we have had the joy of baptizing over six hundred converts on this field.

Hungry Hearts

Everywhere the people were open and receptive, hungering

to hear the word of God. In February, March and April we made a great tour with our preachers, covering both the western and eastern portions of the field. On the western tour, in a night meeting at Nagalapuram, the first village we visited, a great crowd gathered. The young men of the congregation were to the front with eager faces and receptive minds. In the early days of the mission the *Peddalu* (village elders) were old men and often not very bright and shining lights. But now the young men have stepped to the front and assumed responsibility. It is one of the many signs of the New Day in India, and we are glad that it has come. The Telugu loves to sing. And the singing of these young men was remarkable. One of them, a fine young fellow, sang with deep emotion the beautiful Telugu hymn *"siluvanu mositiva - na korakai - kalvari metla paiki."* ("Didst Thou bear the cross for me? Didst Thou climb the steps of Calvery?") The people listened with breathless attention and were deeply moved. And when I made appeal for decisions, fourteen took their stand for Christ. This was the beginning of a great ingathering, the first fruits of the harvest that was to come.

As we went from village to village, holding evangelistic meetings every night, we pitched our tent one day in Pedda Maradi, a village some forty miles from Kurnool. Though touring constantly on the Kurnool field, I had never visited that village before, but preacher Ramiah had been working there and reported that the people were ready for baptism. So we went there that day. The school was held in *Maramma's* temple, a rude structure with mud walls and flat roof and it was crowded with bright little boys and girls with their faces turned toward the light. In the afternoon we preached in the bazaar to a large gathering of Sudras who listened to the Gospel message with absorbing interest. At the night meeting a great crowd gathered and twenty young men rose and confessed Christ. The next morning, in the presence of a great crowd of *Sudra* people, with hymns of praise and fervent prayer, we baptized these fine young men in the name of the Father and the Son and the Holy Ghost—the first fruits of the Gospel in those distant parts.

On the eastern tour one night we were holding a Gospel meeting at Vaddaman, a village twenty miles from Kurnool. The whole *palem* gathered to hear the word of God. Deep interest was manifested. And when we called upon them to take their stand for Christ, there was an immediate response. One after another stood up, mostly young men, until twenty had confessed Christ. It was an inspiring sight and we praised God. When we suggested that they might come to Kurnool for baptism, like the Ethiopian of old they said, "Why wait? Baptize us now." So early next morning we led them down to the Kurnool-Cuddapah Canal and there baptized twenty-eight men and women. So eager were they that even while we were performing the ceremony, some came running, beseeching us to baptize them. That was the decisive hour in the life of those people. Not many days afterwards the Vaddaman Baptist Church was organized and has grown to be a strong and aggressive church, shining like a star in the darkness of the night.

Perhaps the most remarkable meetings on this tour were at Musalimudagu, where a movement to Christianity began the previous year. Here there is a group of five villages. Arriving Sunday morning, we found preacher Rungiah and the Christians eagerly awaiting us. In the afternoon we preached in the bazaar to a great crowd of Sudras who listened to the Gospel message with deep attention. At night the whole *palem* gathered to hear the word of God. The singing of these new converts was remarkable. A great work of grace was going on here. Forty men and women were ready for baptism. The next day we visited Ganapuram. The people had erected a little *pandal* (shed) and decorated it with mango leaves. A table, a chair and a Bible were placed in readiness for us. The people were keen and eager and when we called for decisions, thirty men and women took their stand for Christ. On the third day delegations came to Musalimudagu from Ganapuram, Singarazapalle, Sivapuram and Durgam. After examining the candidates we had the joy of baptizing sixty-three happy converts. At night we observed the Lord's Supper. With great joy and deep reverence the new converts gathered about the Lord's table and for the first time in their lives partook of the bread and the wine—the sacred emblems of His love. As I looked upon that group of humble followers of the Lord Jesus gathered about His table far off in the wilds of India, I thought of the words of the Master, "And they shall come from the East and the West and from the North and the South and shall sit down with Abraham and Isaac and Jacob in the Kingdom of my Father."

On this tour of two months and fifteen days, we visited seventy-two villages, held revival meetings every night and many meetings during the day, baptized two hundred and eighty-one converts and preached the Gospel to great crowds of Sudras.

Wonderful transformations were taking place. One example among many, may suffice. Jolapuram was the home of drunkards and a den of thieves. The old *Maramma* temple under the banyan tree was deserted and a little white-walled Christian chapel was the center of a new life. On Christmas day these people invited us to celebrate the festival with them. We shall never forget the sight of their bright, happy faces, shining with a new love and kindled with a new joy. Christmas had a new meaning as we looked into their faces, for in those humble hearts the Christ was born again!

Our report for 1915 closed with a triumphant note. That year the revival reached its culminating point:

Four hundred and seventy-three baptisms in a single year is something unprecedented in the history of the Kurnool Mission. Eleven new villages have come over to Christianity. In the past three years we have had the joy of baptizing over one thousand converts on this field. Our church membership has more than doubled within this period and has now passed the two thousand mark! This revival movement is gaining force and intensity and we know not what the end will be. God is in it and He is stretching forth His arm to save.

The most significant and far-reaching outcome of the great awakening among the outcastes was the birth of two new churches on the Kurnool field—one a village church and the other the Kurnool town church.

The Kodumur Village Church

The Kodumur church had a remarkable history. For years we had preached the Gospel in that village, but this old stronghold of Satan stood unmoved and seemingly unmovable. But at last the revival came, and swept over those parts. We were on tour in Kodumur, holding evangelistic meetings. In the meeting that night twenty-six men and women rose and confessed Christ, and the next morning we baptized them in the Handri River. We determined to follow up the work at once. At the very next *nelasary* we appointed Rev. Reddipogu Ezra, one of our best preachers, to Kodumur to instruct the new converts in the things of Christ. Their progress in the Christian life was phenominal. When I visited Kodumur one year later on Saturday night we had a public meeting with a special program of songs, addresses, scripture verses etc. arranged by the pastor. The singing of the people was something wonderful. I have never heard anything like it in India. The men sang, then the women sang, and then the school children. Each group seemed to excel the other. The school children were all dressed in their Sunday-go-to-meeting clothes their faces were bright and shining with a new light. They looked like caste children. The village *Reddi* (magistrate) was present at the meeting and I called on him to speak. He responded by saying that these people, once outcaste *Madigas,* were conmpletely changed since becoming Christians. During the meeting one of the *peddalu* rose and said that he would like to make a request. I supposed he was going to ask for help of some kind. What was my surprise to hear him request that they might have a *church* in their village! So on the twenty-fifth day of May, 1918, the Kodumur Baptist church was organized with a membership of over one hundred. Inspiring services were held Saturday and Sunday with delegates and Christians from many villages. What added special significance to the event was the fact that these people were not Christians of thirty or forty years standing. Five years ago they were all heathen, bowing down to dumb idols. But so eager and earnest were they that they had outstripped many older Christians and pressed on to the attainment of corporate church life. Though poor in this world's goods, struggling for a livelihood by carrying head-loads of fire-wood to the market, they pledged one-half of the support of their pastor and as an earnest proof of the same, laid down on the table twenty-eight rupees! Would not the Master say, as of old, "Verily, these too are sons of the Kingdom"? That day was a day of great rejoicing.

Kurnool Town Church

That same year, on September 1, the Kurnool town church was organized. Hitherto the Christians of Kurnool town and surrounding villages had been merged in the mission field church, without a separate and distant church life to draw out their activities and to bring them to a realization of their duties and responsibilities as Christians. After much prayer and deliberation, therefore, they resolved to organize themselves into a separate church for aggressive Christian work. Delegates were invited from all the churches in the association and a large and representative gathering assembled. Sunday morning, Dr. John A. Curtis, our missionary at Donakonda, preached an inspiring sermon on "The Church," after which the Church Council of delegates met with Rev. R. Matthew of Ramapatnam Seminary, as Chairman and the new church was duly organized, choosing Rev. Dwaram Chinna Lingayya as pastor and electing deacons and officers. Solemn charges were given to the pastor, to the church and to the officers, by the Kurnool missionary, Dr. Curtis and Rev. Matthew, respectively. In the afternoon sixteen happy believers were received into the church by baptism. After this joyful ingathering of new converts the pastor preached his first sermon to the church, after which he led them to the Lord's Table in a very tender and impressive service. It was a season of great spiritual uplift to all assembled. Writing of this great event in our report of 1918 we said:

> The pastor, Rev. Dwaram Chinna Lingayya, is one of our strong young men, beloved and esteemed by all, a graduate of our high school and a recent graduate of the Ramapatnam Theological Seminary in the Advanced course. He enters upon his duties with enthusiasm and with high hopes. A great opportunity awaits the church. It is the fruitage of long years of toil and effort on this field and marks a new step in advance in the progress of the Kingdom of God in these parts.

With great fidelity and unfailing devotion Rev. D. C. Lingayya served the church as pastor for twenty-three years, until his resignation in 1941. He was succeeded in the pastorate by Mr. Reddipogu David, pastor of the Gudur Baptist Church, one of our beloved "boys", who has already made a large place for himself both in the church and in the community.

IX

JOURNEY TO THE NORTH: LENGTHENING THE CORDS

AFTER worshiping for twenty-five years in the little Rogers Memorial Gospel Hall and for several years in the high school auditorium and after the Kurnool town church was organized as a separate and distinct body, we sorely felt the need of a house of worship for our growing Christian community and as a center for evangelistic work in the town and district. In response to our request our beloved friend and benefactor, Dr. Coles, entered heartily into our plans for the erection of a commodious and beautiful church building in Kurnool.

Coles Centennial Memorial Church

One of the finest sites in the town, opposite the Coles Memorial High School and on the main thoroughfare of the town, was secured at a cost of Rs 4,500, which amount was cabled to us by Dr. Coles. On November 3, 1917, the foundation stone was laid by our beloved senior missionary in the district, Dr. John Newcomb of Cumbum, in the presence of a distinguished company of Hindu and Mohammedan gentlemen and a great concourse of our Christian people.

The work of construction was greatly delayed by the war, which made building operations well-nigh impossible, but at last after innumerable delays, the great building was completed and the last stone laid. On September 21, 1919, in the presence of a great assembly of the Telugu Baptist Convention, a large and representative gathering of missionaries and eager throngs of our Christians from all over the field (a concourse numbering more than two thousand Telugu Christians) the Coles Centennial Church was dedicated in a solemn and uplifting service of prayer, praise and worship, to the glory of God and the advancement of His Kingdom in India.

The church building, pronounced by competent authorities to be one of the most beautiful church edifices in India, is Gothic in design, spanned by lofty arches and adorned with beautiful rose windows in the gables and chancel. It is flanked by a magnificent tower, rising over one hundred feet above the ground and equipped with a tower clock and bell sent out from America by Dr. Coles as a special gift, with an inscription of his own design. Constructed of our beautiful Kurnool limestone, every stone chisel-dressed, the total cost of the memorial church, including site and equipment, was Rs 60,000 ($20,000) a paltry sum for so magnificent a building which in America would have cost many times that.

In front of the church is an impressive bronze bust of Dr. Coles on a marble base, erected at a cost of Rs 2,000 by the free-will offerings of the Christians of Kurnool town and district and other friends of the mission, Hindu and Mohammedan, who as boys studied in the Coles Memorial High School. The unveiling ceremony was performed by Dr. Joseph C. Robbins, Foreign Secretary of the American Baptist Foreign Mission Society, in the presence of a distinguished gathering of Hindu and Mohammedan gentlemen of the town and district. Dr. Robbins delivered on the occasion an inspiring address on Dr. Coles, in recognition of his munificent gifts to the cause of foreign missions in India.

On a marble tablet within the walls of the church is placed, in accordance with the wish of Dr. Coles, the following inscription:

Coles Centennial Memorial Church, gift of Dr. J. Ackerman Coles of Scotch Plains, N. J. Erected in 1919 as a memorial to a century of American Foreign Missions in India, 1813-1913. One of the most beautiful churches in South India.

THE COLES CENTENNIAL CHURCH
THE GIFT OF J. ACKERMAN COLES, M. D.., L.L.D.
IN RECOGNITION OF DIVINE POWER
REVEALED IN THE BEGINNING AND GROWTH OF
AMERICAN FOREIGN MISSIONS, 1813-1913
ALSO IN REMEMBRANCE OF HIS FATHER
ABRAHAM COLES, M. D. Ph D. L.L.D.
AND OF HIS MOTHER, CAROLINE ACKERMAN COLES
AND OF ALL WHO LIKE THEM HAVE BEEN IDENTIFIED
THEREWITH

This inscription expresses in beautiful language the significance of this memorial church. It is a gift of love, It is a memorial to a great enterprise, it is a temple of the living God. As men look on its lofty spires and enter its open courts, our prayer is that they may hear and heed its message—the joyful message the angels brought to this sad earth when Christ, the Saviour, was born: "Behold I bring you good tidings of great joy, which shall be to all people; for unto you is born this day in the city of David a Saviour, which is Christ, the Lord."

In Perils Oft

The missionary life often calls for stern decisions. One of these confronted us in 1917. Fanny and I decided that the time had come to take the children to the homeland. "Ed" had passed his Senior Cambridge examination at Breeks Memorial School, and Katharine was well along at Hebron, Coonoor. As I could not leave India until the Coles Memorial Church was completed, this step involved separation of our little family. Accordingly in February of that year I accompanied Fanny and the children to Colombo to assist them in embarking for America. The First World War was then at its height. The very morning we arrived in Colombo the startling news was received that the Bibby liner, S.S. *Worcestershire*" had been sunk the night before just outside the harbor. Three days later, on the very day that Fanny and the children were to sail, the news came of the sinking of another liner in practically the same place! In the face of such alarming conditions I did not dare to send the family over the perilous seas. So I brought them back at once to Coonoor, thanking God that there was a place where they could remain in safety.

After spending the hot season at the Hills, on September 1 they sailed from Madras for America. To see them safely over the danger zone, so to speak, I accompanied them to Singapore, putting them safely on board ship for Hongkong and returning to Madras by the next steamer. On November 3 I received a cable announcing their safe arrival in San Francisco. For God's protecting hand in bearing them safely over the perilous seas and permitting them to see once more the loved one in the homeland, we shall never cease to be thankful. In the meantime I held on alone, not despairing of a better day. After two years of strenuous labour, the Coles Memorial Church was completed and dedicated. With the completion of this great undertaking, I felt free to turn my face toward the homeland.

Before sailing there was one thing that I wanted to do. Though we had spent nearly thirty years in India, we had never found time in our busy missionary life to visit the great historic cities of North India. I determined, therefore, to do so now. As I was to sail from Bombay on November 7, the time was limited and much of interest had to be cut out. But in a twelve days' tour of the North I saw some of the high lights of India.

Benares—Sacred City of the Hindus

From Bombay I went directly to Benares, Sacred City of the Hindus on the banks of the Ganges River. "Mother Ganga," as the Hindus love to call the Ganges, is a broad and majestic river, sweeping around the city in a great curve. The banks of the river are lined for miles with the palaces of Indian princes and with countless temples dedicated to Hindu gods. At the water's edge are bathing ghats for pilgrims and burning ghats, where corpses are cremated and the ashes strewn on the sacred waters. At sunrise I saw a marvellous sight—myriads of pilgrims bathing in the sacred waters, chanting their prayers, strewing garlands of flowers on the bosom of "Mother Ganga" and immersing themselves in the holy waters, vainly striving to wash away their sins.

From the river I went to the Golden Temple of Siva, the most sacred temple in Benares. Through narrow, winding lanes, reeking with mud and water from the feet of myriads of pilgrims, I entered the Golden Temple. A ceaseless stream of pilgrims was pouring into the inner court of the temple—myriads of devotees, their garments dripping with the water of the sacred river, prostrating themselves before the golden image of the great god Siva! Here was Hinduism—the utter devotion of a great people a devotion that has survived through all the vicissitudes of time, the shock of invasion, the rise and fall of empires, the impact of Western civilization, and still survives, after forty centuries! It is this that makes India great. If only this devotion, this *bhakti,* as the Hindus call it, were laid at the feet of our Christ it would be the dawn of a new day for the fair land of *BHARATA.* For this we labour and pray!

Agra and the Taj

From Benares I passed through Allahabad, capital of the united provinces, and Cawnpore, great cities pulsing with the life and energy of the mighty North. Thence on to Agra and the Taj. Arriving at five in the morning, I could scarcely wait for the great event. After a hurried breakfast, I took a *tonga* and started out on the great quest. The approach to the Taj is through a beautiful park, along a winding driveway, giving one a premonition of the great vision which is to come. The entrance is through a noble gateway of red sandstone, trimmed with marble, and then the sight of the Taj bursts upon you. No disappointment here! A vision of beauty and loveliness unsurpassed in pure white marble! A magnificent dome and minarets—the whole set in a beautiful garden with fountains playing in the sunlight!

As one draws nearer the exquisite workmanship appears. The marble is inlaid with precious stones, fashioned in floral designs in the most exquisite forms. Inside is the incomporable marble screen, wrought with the delicacy of embroidery, encircling the tombs of Emperor Shah Jehan and his beloved Queen, Mumtaz-i-Mahal, in whose memory this glorious monument was erected. I lingered long about the enchanted place drinking in its beauty and seeking to grasp its every detail. It is like a jewel, with workmanship so fine and delicate and artistic. Well may it be said of the creators of this masterpiece: "They began like Titans and finished like Jewellers."

The next morning I was up bright and early and rushed to the Taj to see it by sunrise. With the rays of the rising sun shining upon it, the Taj was gloriously reflected in the waters of the Jumna River on the banks of which it stands. The sight was one I shall never forget. I lingered long and viewed it from every side, climbing one of the tall minarets. Everywhere there was beauty. The Taj grows upon one the longer one looks upon it. It is in truth one of the wonders of the world—a poem in marble!

In the afternoon I went to the fort built by Akbar and the palaces built by Shah Jehan. The Pearl Mosque is of entrancing beauty—one of the architectural gems of the world.

The Taj Mahal – "A Poem in Marble"

There also is the Hall of Private Audience where the Emperor sat upon his Peacock Throne in dazzling glory, the fish pond where he fished, the seat from which he watched the elephants fight below, the baths of the queens with mirrors in the walls, the gardens and fountains, the palaces of Akbar's Hindu wives and the beautiful Jasmine Tower, where the Emperor passed his last hours, a prisoner in his own palace, wistfully gazing on the domes and minarets of the Taj far down the Jumna River. A marvelous sight of grandeur and departed glory! After I had seen this, I felt that I had seen all. Nothing could surpass it!

Imperial Delhi

From Agra I went to Delhi, historic city, ancient capital of the Mogul Empire. Though the old emperors, Akbar and Shah Jehan and all the rest, have long since passed away, Delhi still remains a great Moslem city, center of Islamic life and culture. One of the most impressive sights in the city is the *Jamma Masjit,* the great Moslem mosque of Delhi. When I arrived there, it was the hour of *namaz* (prayer). The open court in front of the mosque was filled with a vast assembly of worshippers. There must have been at least a thousand, kneeling on their prayer rugs, their faces turned toward Mecca, prostrating themselves upon the ground, repeating the sacred words of the Koran and the names of God, *"Allah Akbar"* (God is Great). An impressive and moving sight it was. Here was *Islam,* the religion of the Prophet which has swept in conquering power over half the world, still strong, vital and aggressive.

The center of attraction in Old Delhi is the fort, built by Emperor Shah Jehan, the great builder. Surrounded by a massive wall, the interior is laid out elaborately with the palaces and buildings of state. Here in imposing array are the Hall of Public Audience, the Hall of Private Audience, the beautiful mosque for the special use of the Emperor and his Queen, the private apartment of the Queen and many other buildings. The most beautiful and imposing structure is the Hall of Private Audience with its elaborately carved marble pillars, its rich inlaid work and its ceilings decorated with silver and gold. Over all is the famous inscription: *"If there be anywhere on earth a Paradise, it is here, it is here."*

But the proud emperors who built it have passed away and the marble halls are empty and falling in ruins!

Taking a *tonga* in the afternoon, I rode out twelve miles from Delhi on the Lahore Road to the *Kutub Minar,* the great watch tower built by Mohammed Ghar, founder of the Mogul Empire, in the thirteenth century. Climbing the two hundred and seventy-six steps of the great tower, a magnificent panorama spread out before me. Far in the distance I could see the ruins of seven Delhis, marking the rise and fall of seven great empires. Everywhere was the dust of buried kings and the mausoleums of mighty men of old. And far off in the distance, gleaming in the bright sunshine, were the stately domes and minarets of New Delhi, marking Britain's empire in India.

Jaipur—Native State

The next and last stop was at Jaipur, capital of the Indian state of that name. As the Indian states, numbering over six hundred and comprising one third of the territory and one fourth of the population of India, occupy an important and strategic position in Indian national life, I was anxious to see one of them at first hand. Jaipur is a beautiful city of broad streets and luxurious gardens. It boasts a museum of Indian antiquities, a zoological garden with magnificent specimens of royal Bengal tigers and a sanskrit college for the study of Indian philosophy and oriental religions. The Maharaja is an enlightened ruler, administering his state for the benefit of his subjects. His palace is an imposing structure in the center of the city, constructed of pink sandstone, which gives it a very oriental and bazaar appearance.

The next morning I arrived in Bombay. Thus ended my tour of the great cities of the North. These never-to-be-forgotten days brought to me a new and deeper appreciation of the greatness and glory of India and a new desire to serve her with all my might.

Furlough—1920-21

On November 7, I sailed from Bombay on the old S.S. "Castalia," bound for the United States of America arriving in New York on December 24, just in time for Christmas. Fanny and the children were eagerly awaiting my arrival. After a separation of more than two years, and that in the midst of a great war, you can imagine our joy in being once more re-united as a family. On the urgent request of our daughter Betty, who was married and settled in Southern California, we journeyed across the continent and took up our abode in that delightful clime. Two important events took place during this furlough. First, our son Ed, on passing his examination in Washington, was appointed to the United States consular service and on May 25, 1921, he sailed for China—envoy of good will to the Far East. Second, through the kind invitation of Dr. Samuel J. Skevington, beloved servant of God and pastor of the Hollywood Baptist Church, Fanny and I were taken into the fold of the church and became their missionaries on the Kurnool field. This relationship was to mean much both to them and to us, among other things the gift of a Ford car to carry the Gospel over the rough roads and across the wide stretches of the Kurnool field.

Evangelism—The Primal Task

Returning to India on September 30, 1921, in the stirring times of Gandhi's Non-cooperation movement, we determined to give ourselves as never before to the preaching of the Gospel. The pioneers of the Telugu Mission, Jewett and Clough, were great evangelists, embued with the evangelistic fervor and passion. They were men of vision and daring, ever pressing on into the "regions beyond." One cannot but marvel at the bold and impetuous spirit which led Clough, away back in 1876, with his little band of preachers on that great tour from Ongole to Kurnool, a distance of one hundred and eighty miles. He went across the plains and over the rugged Nalamalla Hills in an ox-cart, opening up a new station on that far western border and planting at Atmakur a little church of twenty-six members which is still the "Mother" church on the Kurnool field! It was faith and vision that wrought these things. Sometimes we wonder if we in these days of mission organization, of committees and offices, of wheels within wheels, have not lost much of that spirit. We realize that conditions are far different today and that the great ingathering in the Telugu Mission (bringing in its wake congregations and churches, schools and institutions which must be cared for and supervised) has laid on every missionary a heavy responsibility and has diverted his energy in some measure at least from the primal work of evangelism. But the missionary must ever be on his guard lest, as the Master said to Martha, he become "distracted" about many things and lose the "better part." The missionary must still be an evangelist, if indeed he have an evangel.

The Good News of Jesus Christ

One of the delightful experiences of the missionary life is

that of taking the Gospel to the people in the villages. It is the joy of seed sowing. It is the deep delight of imparting to men the good news of Jesus Christ. It is the wonderful experience of witnessing the response of the human heart to the Divine appeal. The Gospel we preach is not a doctrine, a theology, a philosophy. It is the good news of God's Love in Jesus Christ. It is something "New" and something "Good". The Hindu has three hundred and thirty-three million gods—more gods than people—but he never heard of a God of Love who gave Himself to save His creatures. This is indeed news to this man and eagerly he drinks it in. How many times have I heard him say, after hearing the message: *"Ayya, idi kotta samacharam"* ("Sir, this is something new").

When I went out to India in the early days, I wondered if the people would understand my message. I was a man of a different race and nation. I was bringing them a new religion—strange and incredible. Would they grasp it? Would they understand it? I had many doubts. But as I stood in the bazaar and talked to them quietly and gently, as man to man, about God—the one true God, creator of heaven and earth, father of all mankind; about sin—this evil thing in our hearts; and about salvation—the way of deliverance, I could see as I looked into their faces that they understood. When I finished they would say: *"Ayya, idi satyamaina samacharam"* ("Sir, what you say is true"). Then and there I learnt the great lesson that the heart of man is the same the wide world over. It matters not what the race or colour or language may be. Deep down in his heart he is a man like myself—a sinner in need of God! I came to know that the word of God is a living seed and the heart of man is the soil, and if the seed be cast into that soil it will spring up and bear an abundant harvest!

Now how do we get this good news of God's love to the people? Here in America you open the doors of your churches, switch on the electric lights and start the organ and the people come. (And some times they don't come.) But you can't do that out in India. You can't expect the people to come to you. They don't know who you are or what you are doing and they are a bit afraid of the white man. You must go to the people. *You* must take the Gospel to them. And where are the people? Out in the villages. India is a land of villages. There are only a few great cities in India—Bombay, Madras, Calcutta, Delhi, Lahore, Hyderabad. There are 700,000 villages in India, each with a population of from 500 to 5,000. There you will find the people. And if you would reach them, you must tour the villages. When I first went out to India, one day I was reading my New Testament and I came to the passage where it says, "And Jesus went about through all the villages of Judea and Samaria and Galilee, preaching the Gospel of the Kingdom." On the Sabbath day Jesus was wont to go to the synagogue, but all the other days He was going from village to village and from house to house, in the bazaars and the market-places, by the seaside and in the temple courts, wherever men were to be found. This was Jesus' *method.* He was messenger of the grace of God to needy souls everywhere. As I read the wonderful story anew, I said to myself, "It is enough for me to follow in His train."

After our return to India from the homeland, with joy we took up this work. Practically the whole of March and April, 1922, was spent on tour. Both the eastern and western portions of the field were covered and nearly every Christian village was visited. It was delightful to be among our people once more and to see their joy and steadfast faith. The *Sudras* seemed more ready and eager to hear the Gospel message than ever before. Great crowds gathered in every place and listened to the message with deep and absorbing interest. On this tour we visited thirty-five villages, held fifty-six meetings, baptized one hundred and six converts and preached the Gospel to great crowds of people. In October and November, when the rains were over, we spent nearly every week-end in the villages, holding meetings and baptizing converts. A great harvest was reaped and by the end of the year three hundred forty-six converts were baptized, the largest number, with one exception, ever baptized on this field in a single year.

Rangamma of Jalkanur

A very remarkable work sprang up during the year in one of the villages on the Kurnool field. In the month of September we heard that there was a Christian woman in Jalkanur who was healing the sick by prayer. At first we did not give much credence to the report, but the work continued to grow week by week, great crowds of people coming to be healed. At last in October we went out to see for ourselves. We found a quiet little woman, Rangamma by name, uneducated and unlettered, with no pretensions of any kind and apparently possessed of no remarkable traits. Sitting at the door of my tent, she told her story. She was a widow and had been a Christian about ten years. Even after becoming a Christian, for some years she continued to worship the family idols in the house. One day as she was returning to her house, thinking about these things, she saw a bright light and heard a voice saying, "Rangamma, do you believe in me or do you believe in the idols?"

"Lord", she said, "Thou knowest that I believe in Thee."

"Then," said the voice, "throw away your idols and serve Me only. I will heal."

She went home and cast away her idols and began a new life of faith in Christ. At times as she prayed a strange power possessed her, or, as she explained it, the *Vack* (Word) would come upon her and then she could heal. When the *Vack* left her, the power ceased and she must wait for it to come again. This was her story—*a vision, a changed life and a new power.*

Sunday morning came and we went over to the meeting. To accomodate the crowds, our Christians had built a *pandal* in front of the church. The little chapel and the *pandal* were packed with people, all seated on the floor as closely as they could sit and even the surrounding walls and the tops of the houses were lined with people. The majority were *Sudras* wearing their turbans. All had an eager and expectant look. It was a wonderful sight to see them—people of many castes, seated side by side, drawn to this place from distant villages as by some irresistable power. How eagerly they listened as we preached to them of the Christ, the Divine Saviour, who could heal not only their bodies but their souls as well! After the sermon, the pastor called upon those who had been healed to bear witness. One man said he was nearly blind and his sight had been restored. Another said his leg was covered with sores and so badly swollen that he was unable to walk and he showed us his leg entirely healed. A woman said that her face and hands were so badly swollen that she was not expected to live and she stood before us in perfect health. Many women "possessed" of demons, as they say in India, had been cured and the demons cast out. Then Rangamma took her seat on the chapel steps and began to work. At once there was a rush to get near her and with difficulty the crowd was kept back. As each one came before her, she would ask a few questions and then say, "You will be healed." For several hours this continued. Then suddenly she arose. The *Vack* had left her. Even after this, the people did not go away, but waited patiently for the power to return.

From this time on we went out every week-end to Rangamma's meetings, as we called them. Finally as the crowds grew so great we changed the place of meeting and for two Sundays in succession we had her at Anandapuram and one Sunday at Atmakur. The first Sunday at Anandapuram it began to rain during the service, but the work went right on in the rain. At Atmakur the meetings lasted three days, over a thousand people being present. Many were healed and forty-six persons were baptized.

Writing of this remarkable work at the close of the year we had this to say:

> The work still goes on. The people are coming from all over the field and from distant parts—from Cumbum, Nandyal and the Nizam's dominions. The news of the wonders wrought by this little woman in the name of Jesus is spreading far and wide. A profound impression is being made on the Sudras and many are convinced that the work is of God. A Reddi who was cured of a terrible disease says he is believing and calls himself a Christian. A Kapu woman who was healed of dropsy boldly proclaims her faith in Christ. In Rangamma's own village several Sudra men and women who have been healed regularly attend our services and have identified themselves with our Christians.
>
> What, then, shall we say to this movement? That many, though not all, who have gone to Rangamma, have been healed, seems beyond dispute. The people are here and known and bear witness to the fact. It is difficult to explain these remarkable cures on any natural basis. Away out here in the wilderness in a little village in the heart of India, far from the centers of civilization, unknown even to her own missionary, like the unfolding of a flower in the wilderness this simple, untutored woman becomes possessed of a strange and incomprehensible power and begins to speak with an authority as from above. Crowds flock to her, as they thronged the Master in Gallilee. Scores and hundreds are healed by her word and many thus healed confess their faith in Christ. What shall we say to this?

As Christianity becomes indigenous in India, rooted in the fertile soil of the East, we may expect new and powerful manifestations of its working in the hearts and lives of the people. Something of this kind we seem to see in Rangamma of Jalkanur.

The following year witnessed a great and wide-spread harvest on the Kurnool field. In March and April we toured extensively over the whole field, visiting the churches and congregations and preaching to great crowds of *Sudras* who seemed more open and receptive to the Gospel message than ever before. On this tour we spent thirty-seven days, camped in thirty-nine villages, held seventy-eight meetings and baptized one hundred thirty-five converts. In October and November after the rains, we were out for frequent tours. "Everywhere the fields are white to the harvest," we reported. "The Kingdom of God is at hand for the outcaste in Teluguland." It is not strange therefore that a great harvest was reaped. Most significant of all was the fact that the baptisms were not confined to a few villages, but were widely distributed over the field, no less than forty-seven villages sharing in the harvest. The baptisms for the year numbered four hundred eighty-six, the largest ingathering in a single year in the history of the Kurnool Mission.

The Regions Beyond

"There never was a time in the history of missions in India when the masses of the people, the outcastes and the middle classes, were so open and receptive to the Gospel as today." So we wrote in our reports of 1925. As an illustration of this a remarkable movement towards Christianity sprang up in the Pattikonda Taluk fifty miles west of Kurnool. Here lies a great field of almost virgin soil with one hundred and fifteen villages and a population of over one hundred thousand, a region we had scarcely been able to touch before. In fact I had always felt rather ashamed that we claimed this as our territory, while we were doing so little to work it. We determined therefore, to go in and "possess the land." In a strategic village in that section we placed one of our best evangelists.

Kurnool Jubilee Celebrations, March 4-6, 1927. Over one thousand Christians were present.

The Boy who ran away to become a Christian

His name was Jeradoddi Ramiah—a difficult name for you to pronounce so you may call him just Ramiah. His village was Laddigiri, twenty-five miles from Kurnool. One day as we were preaching the Gospel in that village, this boy was there and heard the word and decided that he wanted this "new religion." A few days later he appeared before me in Kurnool.

"I am Jeradoddi Ramiah of Laddigiri," he said. "I heard you preach in the bazaar the other day in my village and I want to become a Christian."

I looked at the boy in astonishment and said:

"None of your people have become Christians and you are a mere lad. Could you stand alone?"

"Yes, I can," he said.

The boy was so earnest and sincere and so determined that in a few days we baptized him. Then he went back to his village. His old father was a terrible drunkard. When he saw Ramiah, he said:

"Where have you been?"

"To Kurnool," said the boy, "to the missionary who told us about the true God. I have been baptized and am now a Christian."

When the old man heard that, he flew into a violent rage, and seizing a big stick, he beat the boy until the blood ran down his back. But the boy did not cry. He just felt sorry for his old father, for he knew that he did not understand. The boy kept praying for his father and telling him what he knew about God. Early in the morning when he awoke, he would sing one of the beautiful Telugu hymns about *Yesu Swami*. Little by little the old man's heart softened and soon he too believed. One day Ramiah came to Kurnool leading his old father by the hand and he said:

"Sir, this is my father and he wants to become a Christian."

That day we baptized the old man and the boy's face shone with a great joy.

Ramiah entered the boarding school and learned to read and write. He was very earnest in his studies and a very serious minded boy. After a few years he came to me one day and said:

"Sir, I want to go back to my people and tell them about God."

"Stay a little longer in the school and get on with your studies," I said.

"No," he replied, "My people are in darkness and I must go and give them the Light."

The boy was so earnest and determined that at last I consented. Born and reared in a *Madiga palem,* an outcaste, despised by the "twice-born" *Brahmans,* with no learning of the schools, he was taught of God and came to have a deep knowledge of divine things. With a remarkable command of the Telugu language in its purity, a delightful gift of humor and an extraordinary knowledge of the Hindu religion in its popular forms, he became a great preacher and won multitudes of his people to Christ.

No wonder, then, that we chose this man for the big task in Pattikonda. We placed him in Ternakallu, a big village, centrally located, where in days gone by we had preached the Gospel until the stones cried out. Far and wide Ramiah went preaching the Gospel. He was like a flame of fire. A new spirit of power seemed to come upon the man as he went from village to village. Everywhere the people received him with joy. The hearts of the people seemed to be prepared for his message. After two months he came to Kurnool with face aglow and announced that in almost every village the people were believing. This was indeed good news. God was at work. Taking a band of preachers, we started out on the high mission. Great crowds of *Sudras* and outcastes flocked to hear the word. The roads were almost impassible, but we had to get to the people and so we forced the little old Ford car over the rocks and stones and dragged her through the sandy beds of rivers and *vagus* (streams) that we might not miss one hungry soul. On that tour we had the joy of baptizing one hundred and twenty seven converts in nine different villages where there had never been a Christian before. And on a Sunday afternoon from all the surrounding villages these humble followers of the Lord Jesus assembled in the little chapel at Ternakallu, packed to the doors, and for the first time in their lives they gathered about the table of the Lord to commemorate His dying love! "The wilderness and the solitary place shall be glad, and the desert shall rejoice and blossom as the rose."

Touring these parts the following year, everywhere we found signs of the new life. In Palakurti, where there were twenty-six new converts, the little schoolhouse was gaily decorated and some thirty boys and girls were reading in the school. The singing of the men and women was remarkable. The Christians in this village were of exceptional character—a "model village," we called it. In Kadavilla the Christians had built a substantial stone schoolhouse by their own effort and without any financial aid from the mission. They had a prosperous day and night school with twenty-eight pupils on the rolls. The head man of the village, after showing all the work they had done, proudly said: *"Ayya, mamu tsala numminamu."* ("Sir, we have greatly believed.")

Saturday and Sunday we spent in Munugundam, one of the villages that had recently come over to Christianity. The Christians had erected a *pandal* for the occasion and had it gaily decorated with festoons of coloured papers. At night there was a public meeting at which the village *Reddi* presided as chairman and many of the head men of the village were present. Teacher Isaac had prepared a wonderful program of songs by the congregation with the accompaniment of the harmonium. Men, women and children repeated the Lord's Prayer, the Ten Commandments and the Psalms. Dialogues were given by the boys and an address of welcome by the teacher. After this program was presented, I spoke to them on "The New India" as seen in the change wrought in the lives of these outcaste *Madigas*. In closing the meeting the *Reddi* paid a sincere tribute to the progress made by our people since they became Christians.

Sunday was a great day. All of our Christians were present, neatly dressed and with smiling faces. The singing of the congregation was remarkable for new Christians. In the afternoon seventeen new converts were baptized, nearly all young men, making twenty-five Christian families in this village. After receiving the new members into the church, we all gathered about the Lord's table in a very impressive service in which two *Reddis* came and sat by my side and a big crowd of *Sudras* were looking on. As we viewed the solemn scene, we were deeply stirred and the words of the Master came to mind: "The time is fulfilled and the Kingdom of heaven is at hand."

As an outcome of this great movement in Pattikonda, two years later the Ternakall Baptist Church was organized with a membership of one hundred and eighty-three in seven villages, calling as their pastor the devoted man who had led them into the new life. The church, though poor in this world's goods, assumed the full support of their pastor from the beginning and twenty new members were added to the church that very day. All this came to pass in a region where ten years before there was not a Christian!

The Tiger of Veldurthi

Following hard on this movement in Pattikonda was a

further extension of the work in the villages to the south of Kurnool. Here lies the Dhone Taluk, extending sixty miles to the south, with one hundred and twenty villages and a population of a hundred and thirty thousand, where there was scarcely a Christian and where the name of Christ had hardly been heard. With three great *taluks* in the Kurnool field having a population of four hundred thousand, we had never been able to work this section in an adequate way. We determined, therefore, that this should no longer be. In May we placed an evangelist at Veldurthi, the largest and most important village in those parts. The people received him gladly and soon became deeply interested in the "new religion." But a grave obstacle stood in their way. Rama Reddi, the village magistrate of Veldurthi was a rich and powerful landlord and a bitter opponent of Christianity. The outcaste *Madigas* in the village were virtually his slaves, working his lands, servants in his house, hopelessly bound to him by ruinous debts and abjectly dependent upon him for their food and clothing and their very existence. They were mere chattels in his hands. He was known everywhere as the *Pedda Pulli* the "Tiger of Veldurthi" and they trembled at his word. What, then, would happen to the poor *Madigas* if they joined the new religion? The *Reddi* would beat them, perhaps kill them or drive them out of the village or cast them into prison. So they feared. For many days they argued and discussed the matter. Finally a young man in the *palem,* to whom we gave the name of John, in the face of bitter opposition from his father and mother and relatives, boldly took his stand for Christ and challenged his people to follow him. This was the turning point. Casting all fear aside, fourteen men took their stand with him and at our September *nelasary* came to Kurnool and were baptized.

In October we camped in Veldurthi in the little rest house just outside the village. In the afternoon we visited the homes of the Christians, recently received into the church. They welcomed us with joy and garlanded us with flowers. The *Madiga palem* in Veldurthi is one of the largest I have ever seen, with more than one hundred houses, crowded and teeming with people. We realized that here was a great center for Christian work. After visiting the people in their homes, we returned to the rest house and were astonished to find none other than *Rama Reddi* waiting to see us! The Tiger of Veldurthi was as gentle as a lamb! The man who had fought Christianity and terrorized our people was now happy to have the *Madigas* become Christians! Rama Reddi was a man of about sixty-five years, a graduate of the Madras University and a man of great power and influence in those parts. He became very friendly and before we left the village, he promised to give us a fine site for our chapel and school-house. So wonderfully did God change the heart of this man! In the four days we were in Veldurthi we preached the Gospel in all the villages within a radius of ten miles and the people were deeply stirred with the message. Every night in the *palem,* under a big gas light set up by our people, we held evangelistic meetings. Night after night, crowds of three or four hundred people—Hindus, Mohammedans, *Madigas* and our Christians—gathered to hear the Word. The singing of the new converts was inspiring and the people listened to the Gospel message with deep and absorbing interest.

Sunday was a great day. The Christians had erected a big *pandal* in front of the school house and decorated it with mango and plantain leaves. It looked very grand. A great crowd gathered from Veldurthi and the surrounding villages. I preached to them on the "Hidden Treasure" and they drank in the message eagerly. After the service, the candidates for baptism were examined. They came forward eagerly, men and women, old and young, giving good testimonies. There were thirty-five from Veldurthi, four from Nayakallu and three from Bommareddipalle–forty-two in all. In the presence of a great crowd of Hindus and Mohammedans, we baptized them with joy in the village well. After the baptism, with deep solemnity the new converts gathered about the Lord's Table for the first time in their lives to commemmorate His dying love.

In this period from 1922 to 1927, as described above, a great movement towards Christianity sprang up in the far regions to the west and south of Kurnool in the Pattikonda and Dhone Taluks. The Gospel was preached far and wide. A great harvest, unprecedented in the history of the Kurnool mission and wide-spread over the whole field, was reaped. In five years over seventeen hundred converts were received by baptism and the church membership on the Kurnool field rose to over four thousand! "The little one shall become a thousand and the small one a strong nation."

X

THE LITTLE THATCHED HUT: CENTER OF LIFE AND LIGHT

OUT there in the *palem* you will find it. It does not look very grand—only a thatched hut, but its walls are white and clean and it is neat and tidy. It is school and chapel both—school by day and chapel by night. A good combination, is it not? Here are the beginnings of the new life. Here little children are gathered from the filth and degradation of the *palem,* washed and cleaned, taught to read and write, and, for the first time in their lives, hear the sweet story of Jesus. Here men and women gather every night, after the day's work is done, and learn to sing and pray and worship the true God. Here light is beginning to dawn on minds long bound in the prison-house. Here new hopes and desires and aspirations are born. Here the good seed of the Kingdom is being planted in the fertile soil of the human heart and is springing up, green and tender, and after many days the harvest will come. You thought this little thatched hut was a cattle-shed. I tell you it is the nursery of the Kingdom, home of Religion, door to new Life.

After taking over the work in Kurnool in 1895, we soon realized the importance of the village school. In the boarding school opened by Mr. Thomssen shortly before our arrival was a little group of boys from the Gadidamudagu village school. They were bright little fellows and made rapid progress in their studies. As the work developed, in a few years, the call came for teachers in the villages. Five of these boys volunteered and went out. Schools were opened, children were gathered in, converts were won and a new impetus was given to the work. In the following year eight more were sent out and year by year others followed. The little school in Gadidamudagu had become the mother of many sons.

Let us, then, take a look at this little school and see what it is like. As we said, it is not very grand—only a rude hut. The walls are made of bamboo tatties or, it may be, of mud and the roof of bamboos covered with grass. The people have built it with their own hands, the whole outfit costing only from three to five dollars in American money. *A school house for three dollars!* Believe it or not. Sometimes when a site cannot be secured, the school is located in Maramma's temple, which belongs by immemorial custom to the *Madigas.* Maramma, seated in her chariot, is rudely pushed aside into a corner and the children take possession. As you enter the schoolroom, the teacher greets you with a low salaam and the children rise and shout at the top of their voices, "Good Morning, Saar." (They are very proud of their English). There are twenty or twenty-five boys and girls present. Some are neatly dressed, the boys with little caps and coats and shorts, the girls in their pretty little *saris* with flowers in their hair. But some of the little tots, alas, are clothed only in sunshine! These children, you must remember, are outcastes, the poorest of the poor. They have never seen a book before or been inside a school. A new world has opened up to them and their bright little faces are turned toward the light. The teacher also is an outcaste, one of their own, but educated and trained in the Kurnool boarding school—now a Christian at work among his own people. In the schoolroom is a table and a chair, or more likely, a stool for the master and a blackboard. The children sit on the floor—no desks or benches out here—and the infants make their Telugu letters in the sand with their fingers! The walls are covered with pictures and drawings and gaily hung with festoons of coloured papers. Very proud they are of their little school, for who ever heard of a school in a *Madiga palem!*

Problems of the Village School

But this little school, so fascinating and so full of hope and cheer, has its problems. First of all is the poverty of the people. The outcaste lives on the border-land of starvation. Every child must contribute to the support of the family. The younger children gather sticks for firewood or herd goats or buffaloes and the older children are hired out to *Sudra* masters for their food and a petty wage. To take a child away from these tasks and put him in school means a real sacrifice. In the second place, these people are utterly illiterate and have no conception of the value of education. Neither they nor their fathers ever went to school. "Why should a *Madiga* read?" they argue. "Can the cobra drink milk?" In the wake of all this, every four or five years famine comes. The rains fail; the crops wither; there is no work. Hunger drives the people from their homes in search of food. Schools are closed and the children scattered like birds in winter time. All your fine plans for the education of the *Madigas* have come to a dead end. These are some of the elements in the problem.

The village school, we must admit, is beset with difficulties. Its problems seem well-nigh insoluable. But however great the difficulties may be, we must continue to struggle with them until they are overcome for the village school is the foundation of our work. Crude though it may be, here the child gets the first taste of an education and it is from the little *palem* school that the graduates of our high schools and colleges come. Here we are at the fountain-head of supplies for the Kingdom and no effort spent on this little school is in vain.

The situation is by no means hopeless. The Christian community is awakening. There is a growing demand for education, a desire for something better and higher. The first request of the people on becoming Christians is for a school and a teacher. This is the fruitage of the new life—the hunger of the heart for light and knowledge. The new wine must needs have new bottles. The new life must express itself in new forms. The people are no longer satisfied with the old life of ignorance and poverty. They want to *rise* and they want their children to *rise*. How eager they are for this little schoolhouse! Out in India the rush is not for Klondyke gold, but for a school and a teacher! This is a situation full of hope and fraught with great possibilities.

In the early days of our work in Kurnool, the schools were few, the supply of workers was scanty and, in the face of oft-recurring famine and pestilence ravaging the villages and scattering the people, the little school had a perpetual struggle for existence. As late as our return to India in 1912, after our second term of service, there were only fifteen schools on the Kurnool field. After seventeen years of labour, we seemed to have made very little progress in solving the problem of a literate Christian community. With the great ingathering of 1913-1915, however, the demand for schools and teachers became imperative and insistent. These "little ones" of the Kingdom, so needy, so hungry, so eager for the light, could not be turned away. *They must be fed.* In our report of 1914 we said:

> The ingathering during the year has led to a marked extension in our village schools. As the new villages have come over to Christianity the demand has invaribly been for a teacher and a school. In response to the call of these hungry souls, we have opened no less than ten new schools. To meet the demand of the new converts for

teachers our force of workers was largely increased during the year. All of our boys in the third and fourth forms of the high school were sent out to care for these needy souls. I have been surprised and astonished at the work of these young men.

The following year, 1915, we reported as follows:

> The problem now is to keep pace with the growth of the work. If this movement continues. I confess I do not know where the workers are coming from to care for these multitudes. We have now 37 village schools on this field, with an enrollment of 982 pupils. Our best schools are manned by husband and wife working together with one mind and heart for the uplifting of their people. It is an inspiring sight. We are most fortunate also in our inspecting officers in the Educational Department who, through **Brahmans,** show a genuine sympathy with our people and a deep interest in this work among the outcastes.

Again in 1931-33 a wide-spread movement towards Christianity led to a great expansion in our village schools. Faced with waiting groups of converts at every *nelasary,* crying, "Give us a teacher," we kept calling for new workers. There never failed to be a response. One young man who had been in government service for many years and had a lucrative post, resigned his position and took up work under our Field Association on a bare pittance. Another young man had built up a splendid school of his own and was earning a large grant, but he was not satisfied with this. He gave up his position and offered himself as a worker. During the year twenty-nine new workers were taken on and still a half dozen villages were calling for teachers.

Breaking the Walls of Caste

One of the most encouraging aspects of the village work is the large number of *Sudra* children attending our schools. They mingle without restraint with the outcaste boys and girls, daily read the Bible, sing our hymns and pray to Jesus. It means a great deal when a *Sudra* man will send his boy to a Christian school. When he is willing to let his boy sit side by side with an outcaste boy and daily study the Bible, it means, on the one hand, that something has come to be more to him than caste and, on the other hand that he has allied himself to some extent at least with Christianity. What this mingling of caste children with outcastes in our village schools and their instruction by a Christian teacher will mean in the days to come, we can but dimly see, but it requires no prophet to say that we are sowing the seeds of a mighty spiritual awakening in India.

Little Rama Reddi

One day on tour in Regadagudur, we were examining the children in Scripture. They were repeating passages from the Bible. In the fourth standard was a bright little *Sudra* boy of the *Reddi* caste, about twelve years old. When it came his turn to recite, he repeated the wonderful words of Isaiah, fifty-third chapter:

> "He was despised and rejected of men, a man of sorrows and acquainted with grief . . . Surely he hath borne our griefs and carried our sorows. He was wounded for our transgressions; he was bruised for our iniquities; the chastisment of our peace was upon him and with his stripes we are healed. All we like sheep have gone astray and the Lord hath laid on him the iniquity of us all."

As little Rama Reddi repeated with great earnestness and deep feeling these inspired words, prophetic of the suffering Christ, I seemed to hear in his voice the cry of a great people for God. During the three days we were in the village little Rama Reddi followed me about wherever I went and on the Sabbath day when we observed the Lord's Supper with our people, the dear little boy sat right by my side, deeply intent upon all that was done. The words of the Master seemed very real to me that day, "Suffer the little children to come unto me and forbid them not, for of such is the Kingdom of heaven."

The Song of Salvation

On tour in the western portion of the Kurnool field, we camped one day in Inagandla, a little village far removed from the haunts of civilization. Strange to say in that village, built on a rocky hill, we had a very fine school with an enrollment of some forty-seven pupils, seventy-five per cent of whom were *Sudra* children. In the afternoon a public meeting was held at which Timma Reddi, the village magistrate, presided. The whole village turned out. Teacher Jacob and his wife put on a wonderful program of songs, recitations, dialogues, and *kolattam,* closing with a drama acted by the fifth standard *Sudra* girls, depicting the change wrought by Christianity in the lives of the people. The remarkable thing about this school was that all the pupils in the fifth standard were not only *Sudras* but girls, and that in a little village school! The parents of these girls, and in fact the whole audience, listened with breathless attention as the leading girl, with a Bible in her hand, sang the great story of Salvation. A profound impression was made. And as the people of Inagandla went to their homes that night, they said to one another: "Some day this song will become true."

Lessons by Lamp-Light

In 1923 a further advance in our educational work in the villages was made by the establishment of night schools. In these schools young men from fifteen to twenty-five years of age, working in the fields during the day, were gathered and taught to read, write, sing and do simple sums. Many of these young men were former pupils in the day school, but were forced to leave school by the stern necessities of life. They were now eagerly seizing the opportunity of studying once more. It was remarkable to see how keen they were and how eager to learn, in many cases buying a lantern and purchasing the oil for the school. In a number of the schools *Sudra* young men were attending and in one case at least a Mohammedan. When I went on tour, wherever there was a night school I would see in the congregation a group of young men, sitting close together, many of them with hymn books in their hands. They sang with all their might and when I preached, though some of the old folks might go to sleep under the sermon, the eyes of these young lads were bright with the light of a new day. That year we reported thirty-three night schools on the field. In the following year, the work of opening and developing night schools was continued with unabated zeal. The teachers were keen and the young men were eager to learn. In our report we said:

These groups of eager young men in the night schools, struggling over their books by the light of a smoking lantern, after a hard day's work in the fields, learning to read their Bibles and to sing from the hymn book and to pray to God, are our crown of rejoicing and our hope for the future. These schools are helping to solve the problem not only of producing a literate Christian community, but of reaching and holding the young men in our churches and congregations. Recently in one of our villages seven young men came forward for baptism. They were all night school boys, who had been led to Christ by a faithful and devoted teacher. In another village, during an epidemic of cholera, when the whole village was terrorized and the people were afraid to go out of their houses at night, these young men gathered nightly with their teacher in the little school house and sang and prayed and read and studied until the whole community was quieted and calmed and even the heathen said, "Your God is the true God."

After many years of experiment and testing, in our report of 1931, we expressed our conviction as to the worth and value of the night school as follows:

For the past nine years we have given special attention to the development of night schools. We believe the night school is the most effective means of producing a literate, Bible reading Christian community. This cannot be accomplished through the day school, simply because the children cannot be kept long enough in the school. They drop out at the end of the second or third standards or stagnate in those standards and soon forget what little they learned. But if there is a night school in the village, even after the children become day laborers, they can take up their education again and complete even the fourth standard. We are beginning to see surprising results in these night schools. Night school young men can now stand up in the meeting and read a chapter from the Bible. Night school boys lead the singing in the congregation. They form the brightest and most active group in the church and soon will be the leaders. In a number of schools, under the instruction of the teacher, they have learned and staged a Biblical drama, taking all the parts and reproducing them in a manner worthy of trained actors. There are, we believe, tremendous possibilities in this movement and in spite of all difficulties we are pressing on with the work.

In 1933, our last year in Kurnool, we reported ninety village schools on the Kurnool field manned by one hundred forty-six teachers, of whom eighty-one were men and sixty-five were women, with an enrollment of 2,534 pupils. The potentialities of this little army of boys and girls no one can measure. The future of Christianity in India is in their hands. These little village schools are the vanguard of the King's army—the trench lines where we "dig in and hold on" until we are ready for further advance.

Making Men out of Untouchables

In the little village school a work of profound significance is going on, quiet and unobtrusive it may be, but far-reaching and revolutionary in its effects. Here light is shining in dark places. Here the good seed of the Kingdom is being sown in tender hearts. Here lives are being changed. A new day has dawned on the outcaste.

The *Madigas* of Purucherla village had become Christians. Their first request was for a teacher and a school. Teacher Prakasham, one of our fine young men was sent. As no site could be secured in the *palem,* the school was opened in Maramma's temple. One day the village *Reddi* came to the *palem* for inspection. When he discovered the school in the temple, he became very angry and said:

"Get out of here, you *Madiga* dogs."

Prakasham protested and said:

"Reddi Garu, we have a right to be here. From time immemorial Maramma's temple belongs to the *Madigas.* Here we worship and here we teach our children."

Upon this the *Reddi* became furious and shouted:

"Your rights! I will see about your rights, you *Madiga* dog!"

Rushing from the temple, the *Reddi* ordered the tom-toms beaten, calling the caste people together for conference. That night a band of *Sudras,* armed with sticks and torches, descended on the helpless *Madigas.* Breaking into their houses and dragging them into the street, they beat the head man until he was unconscious. It was a terrible night for the poor Christians. Then began a fierce persecution of the Christians. No merchant would sell them grain or food. No caste man would draw water for them from the village well. No *dhobie* (washerman) would wash their clothes and no *Sudra* master would give them work. But the brave little band never waivered. They stood firm.

"We will never give up our *Yesu Swami,*" they cried.

Every night they met in Maramma's temple for prayers. They gave up their *toddy* (drink). They abandoned the unclean practice of eating dead meat. They refused to beat the tom-toms in heathen processions and to slaughter the buffaloes at the shrine of heathen gods. They were obedient to their *Sudra* masters in their daily work and faithful in the discharge of all their duties. Little by little they won the respect of their persecutors. Love triumphed over hate.

After a time they decided to build a school house of their own. The old Maramma temple was fast falling to ruins.

They must have a new schoolhouse. I secured a fine site for them just outside the village. But they were poor people. How could they build the house? A bamboo hut they would not have. Nothing but a stone house with terrace roof would satisfy them. But they had no oxen, no carts. Then a strange thing happened. The *Sudras* who once persecuted them and beat them said, "We will help you build the school house." They hauled the stone and gave the beams and bamboos and helped build the house. And when the little schoolhouse was done, they were just as proud as the Christians.

Shortly after this, the *Braham* inspector of schools came to the village for his annual inspection. It was a great day for the Purucherla Christians. The little school house was whitewashed outside and in and gaily decorated with flags and festoons of coloured paper. Inside it was crowded with bright and eager boys and girls, all dressed in their Sunday-go-to-meeting clothes—the boys wearing gay little caps and the girls in their pretty *saris* with flowers in their hair. The village *Reddi,* who once drove them out of Maramma's temple, was there and all the village *Peddalu* who beat them that terrible night—no longer enemies, but friends. The fathers and mothers of the children were crowding around, peering in at the windows and doors, eager to see what their boys and girls would do in the presence of the mighty Brahman!

The *Brahman* inspector called the classes. He had them read. He gave them sums. He saw them march and play games and do action songs. And, wonder of wonders, he even had them sing and repeat Bible verses and bowed his head as they knelt and prayed in the name of Jesus! And when the inspection was over, he wrote in the visitor's book these words:

"The missionaries are making Men out of Untouchables."

That day the *Braham* inspector saw, in the bright and eager faces of those little outcaste boys and girls, the transformation that is taking place in India. Untouchables made into men! Yes, thank God, that is what is going on in India today! Sixty million untouchables are on the march! The little village school out there in the *Madiga palem* has become the birth-place of a nation!

XI

THE INDIGENOUS CHURCH: CHRISTIANITY ROOTED IN THE SOIL OF INDIA

If you would see Christianity in Eastern garb, you must get away from the mission station with its huge institutions supported by foreign funds, out into the villages where the people live. There you will find a neat little chapel, not with western tower and steeple, but with thatched or tiled roof and clean white walls. On a Sunday morning you will find the pastor in his place, the elders sitting well to the front, and a congregation of devout worshippers gathered from the outcastes of India, bowing their heads in prayer, singing of the sweetness of *Yesu Swami's* love and worshipping, not an idol of stone, but the one true God. Here is Christianity, rooted and planted in the soil of India. Here is the seed-bed of the Kingdom from whence spring the living forces of self-propagation and self-expansion.

Planting the Christian Church

The planting and nurture of such churches, modeled after the New Testament pattern, self-directing and self-propagating, is the most important work the missionary has to do. The station churches in our Telugu mission, many of which are situated at important centers, such as Madras, Nellore, Ongole, Kurnool, and Secunderabad, where they minister to large and enlightened congregations, occupy a commanding position in the mission. Many of them have as pastors our strongest and finest young men who are leaders of the people.

Top left: "The Little Thatched Hut," center of light and life. Top right: Dedication of Stanton Memorial Church. Over five hundred Christians were present. Bottom left: Harvest Festival-Regadagudur Church. Bottom right: Village School in Maramma's Temple.

But the station church with its crowds of boarding school boys and girls, its force of mission workers and its imposing buildings, erected either at mission expense or as a gift of some kind friend in America, is not the typical Telugu church. This savours far too much of the west and western organization. If you would see the typical Telugu church you must go out to Gadidamudagu or Regadagudur, to the little village church, with its thatched roof and mud walls and its group of humble village folk. There you have, in that little group of pastor and people and village elders, something indigenous, rooted in the soil and capable of indefinite expansion—both as regards the training of the people and the evangelization of the land.

The Regadagudur Sangham (Church)

Let us, then, go out to Regadagudur (black soil village), a typical Indian village, forty-five miles from Kurnool on the far-confines of the field. There you have the Regadagudur *sangham* (church). You may not be able to pronounce it, but that is simply because you are not a Telugu. It doesn't look much like a church—no steeple and no stained glass windows. It is not very grand with its thatched roof and mud walls, but it is neat and clean and on festival days it is gay with festoons of coloured paper and chains of marigolds and jasmine flowers. The Telugus are very proud of their little church. The pastor is Rev. Reddipogu Ezra, one of our "boys", educated and trained in our Kurnool boarding and high schools and a graduate of the Ramapatnam Theological Seminary. On a Sunday morning you will find all of the people gathered in the little church, a congregation of about one hundred. All are seated on the floor—no benches out here—the women on one side, the men on the other and the children in between. All are dressed in their best—the women in their bright *saris* with flowers in their hair, the men in white *panchas* and flowing robes and the little children in gay jackets and bright little caps. As one thinks of these outcaste people, (beating their tom-toms in wild orgies before their gods and smearing themselves with the blood of goats and buffaloes, slaughtered before heathen shrines) and then sees them here in this little chapel "clothed and in their right mind", worshipping the true God and singing His praises, it seems like a miracle. Yea verily, it *is* a miracle.

The *Brahman* says that the outcaste is incapable of worshiping *Paramatma,* the Supreme Spirit, hence he is not allowed to enter a temple or even to look into the pages of the sacred *Vedas* lest he pollute them. But we say to this man, "You are the child of God. He made you and cares for you and in Christ seeks to save you. Arise and go to your Father and say, 'Father, I have sinned against heaven and in Thy sight and am not worthy to be called Thy son.' " The outcaste has heard this word and, like the prodigal in the far country, he has "come to himself" and has arisen and gone to his Father. His dull mind has been quickened. His hard heart has been broken in penitence and contrition. And he has become a new man in Christ Jesus!

Telugu Singing

The Telugus love to sing. In the early days of Christianity in Teluguland, a high caste *Brahman,* Chaudari Purushotham by name, was won to Christ. A learned Sanskrit scholar, versed in all the lore of the sacred books of the Hindus a poet of rare talent, he became one of the most distinguished converts to Christianity in India. Drawing deeply of the living water from the wells of salvation, he poured out his soul through a lifetime in glorious songs of praise which have become the heritage of the Telugu people. Most of the hymns in our Telugu hymn book were composed by this sainted servant of God. I wish you could hear the Telugus sing that grand hymn, *"parishudha, parishudha, parishudha, prabhuva"* ("Holy, holy, holy, Lord God"); or the Christmas song, *"udayinchinardu krestu-nardu* ("Christ was born today"); or join with them in meditation on the Cross as they sing, *"siluva mositiva na korakai - kalvary mettla pai ki"* ("Didst Thou bear the Cross for me, for me didst climb the steps of Calvary?"). See their faces light up as they sing, with joy, *"vinta galla - na Yesu prema"* ("Wonderous Love of Jesus"), or *"Yesu, ne namamrutham - ma kento ruchi aiya"* ("Jesus' name, how sweet the taste"). We say how sweet the "sound"; the Telugus says, how sweet the "taste." In the East the suppliant lays hold of the feet of the one whom he worships. *"ne cheranamuley nammiti, namiti - ne padambuley pattiti, pattiti"* ("At Thy feet I fall"). The cry of the East to find peace for the soul is sounded in the great hymn, *"yedi na vishranthi - e lokamandu"* ("Where shall I find peace in this world"). And when the Telugu sings the majestic hymn, *"manasa nandam - ponduta kananu - mari a baghyam kala danna,"* ("Heavenly Joy, Greater than all Wealth,") his soul is stirred with a profound emotion.

The Telugus sing by heart. Out in the villages hymn books are rare, for the villagers can't read. The new convert, first of all, learns to sing. The village teacher or preacher repeats the words of one of the simple gospel hymns and the people follow until they know the hymn by heart. This is characteristic of the East. The sacred books of the Hindus (the *Vedas, Puranas, Ramayana* and all the rest) are in poetic form. They are sung in the temples and in the market-place, handed down from father to son, until every child can repeat them. Just so our Telugu Christians learn to sing the gospel story in the words and music of their beautiful hymns. Some of the Telugu hymns are rather long, having twelve or fourteen verses. Here in America if you have to sing more than three or four verses, you are ready to fire the hymn book at the minister. But the Telugus love to sing and they will go right through from the first to the fourteenth verse and the more verses there are the better they like it.

We were holding a meeting one night in Pasapula, a new village, where the people had just become Christians. We asked them if they could sing a hymn. They hesitated. Finally one man started a hymn and all joined eagerly. When we commended them, they started another and another until they had sung twelve hymns. And as they sang their faces lighted up with a new joy. They were drinking in the Gospel.

In Palakurthi village Christianity was at a low ebb. We were about to close the school and give up the village. But one night when we camped in the village, the little band of Christians gathered together, sitting very close to one another, and began to sing. The leader was a young man in the night school. The singing was wonderful, deep and soul-stirring. They seemed to be crying to God as they sang. After hearing this I said, "There is life here; the fire still burns."

Away out in Pattikonda Taluk in Kadavilla village, I found a dear old lady who could sing some eighty hymns by heart. I wonder how many of us could match that? One day one of our Christians from Kulamala, a very devout old man, came to my tent to talk about the "new religion." I asked him if he could sing a hymn. *"Aunayya,"* ("Yes Sir") he said, "I can sing *"Nannu gannayya ravey - na Yesu,"* ("My Jesus, Saviour Dear.") With deep emotion he sang the grand old hymn of the Saviour's love. Thus quietly and mysteriously the gospel is planted in the hearts and lives of these humble followers of the Lord Jesus.

Growth in the Christian Life

These little village churches, far removed from the mission

station, with their groups of devout worshippers ministered to by pastors of their own choosing, are the bright spots on the Kurnool field. In tours over the field I have been impressed with the progress made by our Christians in the knowledge of God's word and their growth in the Christian life. The Sunday morning service in our churches is orderly, reverent and uplifting. The little chapel is white and clean and on special occasions is decorated with festoons of colored paper. The pastor leads the service with dignity and grace. The singing of the people, often accompanied by the harmonium and the violin, is inspiring. Nearly every man, woman and child in the congregation is present. Sunday is a great day in the life of the people. Candidates for baptism are examined with great care, the pastor administering the rite. The Lord's Supper is a very solemn and impressive service and makes a deep appeal to the heart of every believer.

The night meetings in the villages are not less remarkable. The school children recite verses from the Bible, repeating the Psalms, the fifty-third chapter of Isaiah and the thirteenth of First Corinthians—not to mention the Ten Commandments, the Lord's Prayer and the Beatitudes.

Young men from the night school read a chapter from the Bible intelligently and without mistakes. The elders offer prayer, in many cases very remarkable prayers, which only the spirit of God could teach them. Men, women and children repeat Bible stories, telling them in their own words. The women sing the beautiful Telugu hymns which they have learnt by heart. In many of the villages the night school boys give Bible dramas—the story of Joseph, David and Goliath, the Golden Image. These attract great crowds of all classes, sometimes a thousand people sitting entranced far into the night. The wonderful stories of the Bible are brought home vividly and realistically to the hearts and consciences of the people. Our pastors and teachers are doing a great work in instructing the people in the word of God and it is bearing much fruit.

Sunday in the Village of Donkeys

One Sunday we were camped in Gadidamudagu, one of our strong village churches. The little chapel was packed to the doors with a congregation of two hundred or more. In this church there is a splendid group of young men. They were out in full force—some twenty-five or thirty of them—all dressed in their best, with hair neat and tidy. They were clean-cut, bright, intelligent young men, representing the second generation of Christianity in the village. They took the front seats and formed a most attractive and delightful group. They are the leaders in the church. The singing was led by a choir of Gadidamudagu boys, composed of two preachers, one head master, one seminary man, five village teachers and five high school students. The pastor led the singing to the accompaniment of violin, cymbals and drum. The singing was wonderful, the whole congregation joining in. The missionary preached to the eager throng on the "Upper Room," and all hearts were deeply stirred. After the sermon Harvest Festival offerings were taken. One man gave ten rupees, another seven, and others, three, two and one. The meeting closed with a solemn and impressive service in which all gathered about the Lord's Table and reverently partook of the bread and the wine. Here is a transformed community, a real church, abounding in good works. The "Village of Donkeys," for such is its name, has become a community of God's children!

Self-Support

The indigenous church must be self-supporting. Its roots must go deep down into the soil. It must draw its resources, not from foreign subsidies, but from the hearts and lives of the Telugu people. If it is to be strong and independent, standing on its own feet, it must learn to bear burdens and to be responsible for its work. How, then, is self-support to be attained, if indeed it can be attained under such adverse conditions. From our experience of forty years on the Kurnool field, may I offer the following suggestions:

1. Self-support should not be made an end in itself. It is a poor thing to preach to the people. The Telugu Christian, face to face with dire poverty, cannot understand why he should be asked to support his teacher or preacher when there is plenty of money in America. He inevitably thinks that any such demand from you is due either to the hardness of your heart or the meanness of your disposition. The preaching of self-support to the Telugu arouses no response in his heart and makes no appeal. So long as we employ this we are reversing the true order. Self-support is a means and not an end.

2. Self-support cannot be attained by the mission reducing the pastor's salary. This method will result either in starving him out or driving him from his post. The theory that the amount we reduce on his salary will be made up by the people is a pure theory and is not borne out by the facts. The people may even promise to give the amount but very soon they drop off and you will be forced either to make up the deficiency or transfer the man to some other place. Self-support cannot be won by force.

3. There is another and more excellent way. *The people must be taught the duty and privilege of Christian giving as embodied in the tithe.* When you tell the Telugu Christian that he should give to the support of his preacher, he does not see why he should do so. But when you tell him that God is the giver of all, that all he has and all he enjoys comes from God, that of that which God gives to us the tenth

belongs to God and He asks us to give that tenth to Him—when you sit down quietly by the side of this humble Telugu Christian and tell him these things about God and his relation to Him, his heart is touched with a deep emotion, just as yours is, and he responds at once and says, "Yes, it is true." Here, then, is a powerful religious appeal. Here you are dealing with the deep realities of life. You are not asking the man to give a few pice or pennies. You are pointing him to God! You are showing him that he has nothing of his own, that all belongs to God and that God has a right to His own and that it is the sacred duty and privilege of every child of God, however poor he may be, to give of his substance to his heavenly Father. I have yet to meet the Telugu Christian who would not respond to this appeal.

This is the method we have tried to follow for forty years on the Kurnool field. Steadily and persistently, through all these years, in season and out of season, we have taught our people these things. We have said very little about self-support but we have preached everlastingly on the Christian's obligation to give to God.

Moonlight Discussion

This process of education and training in Christian giving, carried on through the years, is vividly set forth in the following incident narrated by my associate, Rev. B. J. Rockwood, while in charge of Kurnool during our furlough in 1921. In his annual report he says:

> I should like to close with a testimony to the high sense of responsibility to God that my be found in many of our village churches. Much of the land that is cultivated by our village Christians belongs to the mission. It is Dr. Stanton's custom to ask the cultivators to give a tenth to the Lord. This money goes first to the support of the local church and the balance is used for extension work. Naturally there is much discussion all over the field as to this tenth. But all

this is a means of education. In one large village where they had a good crop, they were having a heated discussion as to the need of this tithing. I happened to come to the village during the height of this discussion and the pastor called a meeting of all the adults, both men and women, to have me hear the discussion and give advice. It was most interesting to see the crowd in the moonlight, seated on the ground, nursing their knees and silent. Finally one man rose and made a speech against the giving of the tithe. Several followed, but some got up and gave arguments to show why they should give. I kept silent and after a long discussion those who favored giving won the day. The arguments were of a very high order. They pointed out the benefits they had derived from Christianity. They urged that God was the giver of the harvest and so deserved a share. They said they were wholly dependent on the will of God and asked if He had not said in the Bible that those who gave cheerfully would be blessed. As they talked thus, I thought to myself that in no village I had ever seen had I heard common villagers talk so intelligently about God and their relation to Him; and this discussion and this intelligence were made possible by the fact that the tithe was demanded and the pros and cons given until the common man had learned the lesson.

Springs in the Desert

In the first year after our return from furlough in 1922, we reported a wonderful year in Christian giving. The May *nelasary* was a field day in self-support. The harvests were gathered. The people had made their offerings. The contributions exceeded all expectations. We decided therefore, that the time had come to place all of our workers on an indigenous basis. For many years the work on the field had been administered by the Gospel Extension Society. Contributions from the churches and congregations and grants earned by the village schools were turned into the treasury of the Society and from this fund the workers were paid. We resolved now to place all field workers on the pay roll of the Gospel Extension Society. This was done and at the close of the year we found that every field worker, whether preacher, teacher or evangelist, had been supported entirely from funds raised on the field. This outstanding result was due entirely to the great increase in giving on the part of our Christian people. The contributions for the year amounted to Rs 3,776—by far the largest contribution from the Christians of the Kurnool field in the history of the mission.

In the following year an even more notable record was made. We were in the midst of a great ingathering on the field and our resources were taxed to the utmost by the constant demand for teachers—a demand we dared not refuse, so long as a man was available. As these new schools had no income from grant, the salaries of the teachers had to be met from our own funds. More than Rs 500 was thus put into the village school work, over and above the grant earned. In spite of these heavy demands, the work was carried through triumphantly. Not a school was closed for lack of funds and not a village was denied a teacher where a man was available. The contributions of our Christians for the year reached the splendid figure of Rs 4,916—a sum more than one thousand rupees above that of the previous year. The promise of God was fulfilled; "I will make springs in the desert."

Harvest Festivals

The new wine of the Kingdom cannot be kept in the old bottles of heathenism. When the seed springs from the earth, it bursts the old husk and rises in a new form. Life ever clothes itself in fresh garments. Under the Eastern sky and the glorious sun Christianity takes on new forms and expresses itself in new modes. In the early days Christianity in India was austere, somber, forbidding. Her characteristic phrase was "Thou shalt not." The positive and vital note was lacking. But as Christianity finds her home more and more in the hearts of the people, as she becomes really indigenous in the land, she is beginning to express herself in Eastern forms. This is seen in the Harvest Festival which is rapidly taking root among our Christians. India is the home of festivals, pilgrimages, *yathras* (fairs). It was inevitable, therefore, that the Indian Christian should have his festivals. Our great festival of Christmas with its appealing story of the Babe in the Manger and the Star in the East, has captured the heart of India, not merely Christian, but non-Christian as well. And so our Indian Christians have seized upon the harvest time, when the ripe grain has been gathered in and the years' work is done, when the minds of men are filled with thoughts of the goodness and bounty of God, and have made of this season a religious festival. They meet together in the house of God with song and prayer and praise and joyfully lay their offerings on the altar.

These Harvest Festivals are seasons not only of much rejoicing, but also of great spiritual uplift. The little chapels and schoolhouses are gaily decorated with palms and flags and coloured festoons. The people come from all the surrounding villages in great crowds, many Sudras also joining in the festivities. A varied program of songs, dialogues, *kolattam* (musical dance), sermons, addresses, religious dramas and magic lantern lectures are presented to which the people listen with absorbing attention. At one of these festivals a magic lantern lecture on the Life of Christ was given in the Sudra quarter of the village and at least a thousand people gathered to hear it, staying to the very end in the wee hours of the morning. The high point of the festival is reached when the people bring their offerings. Besides cash, baskets of grain and vegetables, fowls, eggs, sheep, goats, *ghee* (butter) and oil are brought and joyfully offered. In one case a man brought a cow which was auctioned off for thirteen rupees. As the gifts are made the enthusiasm runs high. The spirit of Christian fellowship is strong and tender. The giving of the Christians is joyful and hearty. The Harvest Festival has come to stay. It has won the hearts of the people.

At first these festivals were confined to our village churches and important centers. Gradually they have spread over all the field. Our aim has been to secure a contribution from every Christian congregation and an offering of at least one rupee from every Christian family. The appeal has been to the religious instinct. We have asked them to give a thank-offering to God for the mercies of the year. The response on the part of the people has been far beyond our expectation. Not one rupee, but two, three, five and even ten they have given with a joy that makes our hearts glad. In one village a little congregation of sixteen families gave sixty-two rupees, one man bringing a bouncing big sheep that sold for seven rupees. In Palakurthi a cripple, dragging himself along the ground, gave a rupee. A poor woman of Brahmankotkur whose son had been ill gave a thank-offering of fifteen rupees. In a village where the people had just become Christians, we did not think of taking an offering, but one man stood up and asked if they might give their *tsanda* (offering). We assented and he came forward and laid a rupee on the table. Others followed until they had thirteen rupees. In Nayakallu the people were very poor and in the midst of famine. There was no crop and no harvest, but at the night meeting every man came forward and made an offering of one rupee. We would not have dared to ask them for one pice. In many villages the *Sudras* join our Christians in giving and often bring garlands of flowers with the offering.

The mission tank-bed lands in Gadidamudagu were flooded with water from the heavy rains. The crops were completely destroyed. It was a heavy blow to the little church, for these lands were the chief source of income and the Gadidamudagu church in normal times was our largest giver. Undaunted, the Christians determined to hold their Harvest Festival as usual. I wondered what they would do. When the time came to take their offerings, Lakshmiah, the leader among the young men in the church, came forward and placed fifty rupees on the table. I was astonished and so was everyone else. Then another came forward and gave fifteen, several gave ten and the rest five each. At last when all had made their offerings, we counted the money and found two hundred and twenty-six rupees—all from their own lands! A wonderful offering! The flood had destroyed their crops but could not quench their spirit.

A Christian Village

At the close of our tour in May, 1933, the Coles Dharmapuram settlement held its annual Harvest Festival. The families invited their relatives and friends from far and near for the great occasion. The houses were made white and clean. The chapel was gaily decorated with festoons and palms and flowers. The people were dressed in their best. The village had a festive and cheerful aspect. At ten o'clock the whole village gathered in the beautiful chapel with Christians from three surrounding villages to celebrate the Harvest Festival. The little chapel was packed to the doors. Songs were sung. Scripture verses were recited by the school children. Bible stories were told by the congregation. Garlands were presented. A message of joy and praise was given by the missionary. Then the offerings were taken. One man gave twenty rupees, another ten, others five, three, two and one. The pile grew higher and higher on the table. Each one was cheered as he laid his offering on the plate. When all had given, the offerings were counted and the total was seventy-seven rupees—all this in addition to the tithes from their lands. It was a day of great joy and we were glad that here was a Christian village.

Honey Out of the Rock

What, then, is the outcome of all this? The process of education and training in Christian giving, persistently and lovingly pressed home upon the people during all these years, has borne abundant fruit. Beginning forty odd years ago with an annual collection of less than Rs 100, the contributions of our Christians have grown from year to year until in 1933—our last year in India—high water mark was reached. This in spite of a severe financial depression, both at home and on the field. The Kurnool town church headed the list of contributing churches with more than Rs 700. Coles Anandapuram came next with Rs 346. Five churches gave over Rs 200 each and five over Rs 150 each, only one falling below Rs 100 and that one was without a pastor. Eighty-four villages held Harvest Festivals with offerings amounting to Rs 1626. Fifteen substantial chapels and schoolhouses were erected, one costing over Rs 1000—all without one penny of foreign money. The total contributions of the Christians on the Kurnool field for the year 1933, for the support of their pastors, evangelists and teachers, the maintenance of their churches and schools and the extention of the Gospel into the regions beyond, amounted to the magnificent sum or Rs 9800. Had anyone predicted forty years ago that the time would come when the poverty-stricken Telugu Christians would contribute to the spread of the Gospel on any given field of this mission the sum of ten thousand rupees in a single year he would have been declared a visionary and a wild enthusiast! But the vision has been fulfilled and the word of God has been verified: "Ye shall draw honey out of the Rock."

Their Devotion

How the "tenth" movement began on the Kurnool field

away back in 1897; how the famine came and out of the famine the Christians of Gudur promised, as they sowed their seed, to give one tenth of the crop to the Lord, has already been told. On that Sunday, at the harvest time, when they brought their offerings of grain to the house of God, I was present. One young man, Davogi by name, came into the chapel bringing a huge sack of grain on his back. Laying it down before me, he straightened up and with beaming face said: *"idi na bhakti"* ("This is my devotion.") I have never forgotten that. That act was not simply the giving of so much grain. It was the expression of the "devotion" of his heart. As I look back over these forty years and think of the little groups of humble followers of the Lord Jesus scattered all over the Kurnool field, no longer bowing down to sticks and stone but worshipping the one true God whom they have come to know through Christ, the Saviour, bowing their heads in prayer and singing praises to God, bringing their offerings of grain and the first fruits of the harvest to the house of God, building their little chapels and prayer houses with their own hands—as I think of all this I can only say with Davogi of Gudur, "This is their Devotion." Christianity is no longer exotic in India. It is deep-rooted in the hearts and lives of the people. And as the Master said, *"The Gates of Hell shall not prevail against it!"*

XII

INDIAN CHRISTIAN LEADERSHIP: TRAINING WORKERS FOR SERVICE

It is a truism of mission policy to say that if India is ever to be evangelized it must be through the instrumentality of her own sons and daughters. The missionary, however long he may stay in the country and however thoroughly he may identify himself with the people among whom he lives, is after all a foreigner. He cannot escape being a "white man." He belongs to an alien race. The Indian worker, on the other hand, is one of the people. He speaks their language; he thinks their thoughts; he lives their life. Christianity when preached by him and exemplified in his life, ceases to be foreign. It is the Indian worker, born of the soil, one with the people, who must ever be the true witness to his countrymen of the saving power of the Gospel. These humble and devoted men, bearing the heat and burden of the day, receiving a bare pittance, often suffering privation and hardship, carrying the Gospel to every nook and corner of the land, breaking the Bread of Life to hungry souls, shepherding the flock, are the heart and sinews of the missionary enterprise. Wherever the work of a mission is permanent, wherever it takes root and grows, there you will find a strong and efficient force of Indian workers. Without the Indian worker the missionary would labour in vain, gathering at the most only a few scattered converts. The missionary *brings* Christianity to the land; the Indian worker *plants* it.

The first concern, therefore, of every missionary must be the raising of a band of efficient and Spirit-filled workers

South India Mission Conference, Kurnool, 1922. Foreign Secretary, Dr. Joseph C. Robbins, and Mrs. Robbins in the center. Delegates from Burma, Assam and Bengal-Orissa present.

who shall carry the Gospel into every village and hamlet and make Christianity indigenous in the land. The Telugu Mission from its inception has laid great emphasis on the development of a force of indigenous workers. It was through the devoted labours of these men that the great ingathering on the Ongole field took place. They were the ones who taught and trained the multitudes as they came. Without these men no such movement would have been possible and even if it had come, it would have soon faded away. Through all its long and glorious history the strength of the Telugu Mission has been in these devoted men and women, raised up from among the people. In the great enterprise of bringing India to Christ the Indian worker is the key man.

After taking over the work in Kurnool in 1895, we soon realized that the great need was workers—teachers for the village schools, pastors for the churches and evangelists to carry the Gospel to the people. At first we tried to get workers from some of our older mission stations. One man came from Vinukonda, but the water did not agree with him. Another said Kurnool was a *dura dasham* (distant country) and the people were *chonsu vandlu* (wild men) and a third got sick and ran away. After many fruitless attempts we became convinced that we must raise our own workers from the boys and girls on the Kurnool field. This involved the establishment of strong and efficient boarding schools in which the boys and girls could be educated and trained for future service and leadership. We have already told the story of the growth of these schools from a little elementary school of rude village boys to the splendid Coles Memorial High School with over five hundred students. From these schools a steady stream of workers has poured forth into the needy fields about us—teachers for the village schools, pastors for the churches, evangelists for the unreached multitudes and Bible women for the *zenanas*.

The Pastor as Leader

In the development of the indigenous church in India (a church strong and aggressive, able to bear burdens and take responsibility) the primal factor, humanly speaking, is the pastor. Our experience on the Kurnool field has taught us that if the pastor is a strong and tactful leader, winning the loyalty and devotion of his people, the church will grow and prosper. If, on the other hand, the pastor is weak and unable to command the following of his people the church will inevitably sink to a low estate. We need, then, to look well to the qualifications of the pastor. He should be a man of God, separated unto the Gospel, able to impart to his flock spiritual food and to lead them in active Christian service. Though there are exceptions, in general the pastor should be a seminary graduate, called of God and separated to the Gospel ministry. When our boys on the Kurnool field were ready for active service, our practice was to send them out first as teachers in the village schools. In the stress and strain of the village life they had a real testing. Some never rose above the teacher grade. But now and then one, as he toiled in the villages in the midst of needy and suffering souls, heard the call of God. "Whom shall I send and who will go for us." And he said, "Here am I, Lord, send me." Such men became true pastors and shepherds of the flock.

The pastor should have but one task. He should be a full-time preacher, devoting all his energy to the preaching of the Gospel and the shepherding of his flock. The system of teacher-pastors, prevalent in our mission in certain sections, is of doubtful utility. We do not believe that strong and aggressive churches can be built up under this system. If our Telugu churches are to become centers of life and power to the unreached multitudes about them, they must be manned not by school teachers, but by men separated to the Gospel and free to devote mind, heart and soul to the great tasks of the church.

Again, the pastor must have educational qualifications suited to the new day. This ancient land is in a mighty ferment today. The old order is rapidly passing away. A new India is in the making. To meet these new and rapidly changing conditions we need an educated ministry. If we are to meet these new conditions and provide the necessary leaders for the rising Christian community, I believe the time has come when we should have as pastors of our Churches men who have taken the advanced course in the seminary. But it is often said, "It is impossible to get these men into the village work." On the Kurnool field six of our pastors are matriculates and graduates of the seminary in the advanced course. Mr. R. David, recently called to the pastorate of the Kurnool town church to succeed Lingiah, on completing his seminary course went into the village work, gathered the people about him in a group of villages and organized the Vaddaman church, where, during a ministry of ten years, he did an out-standing work. After that he was called to the Gudur church where he worked for five years with marked success. Mr. R. Devanandam, after graduating from the seminary, took up work in a group of villages in a new section of the Kurnool field. Building up a strong congregation, he organized the Veldurthi church, the fifteenth church on the Kurnool field, where he worked efficiently for ten years. He is now pastor of the Regadagudur church. These are facts of deep significance. If the missionary steadily keeps his grip on his men, if he maintains a close contact with them and ever holds up before them the noble ideal of the Christian ministry, we are convinced that it is not impossible to get these men back into the village work. We have a vision, and that not far distant, when all the pastors of the village churches on the Kurnool field will be matriculates and graduates of the seminary in the advanced course.

Is there scope for such men in the villages? We would reply emphatically, "Yes." The village church, if properly organized and developed, forms a magnificent field for Christian service and leadership. Five or ten villages grouped about a central village form the church. In the central village there is a strong Christian community numbering from seventy-five to two hundred. Regular services must be held; instruction in the word of God must be given; the Christian life in each member must be developed; wrong-doers must be punished; sin must be rebuked; the church must be summoned to its tasks and led out into a new consecration and devotion to its Lord. Besides the central congregation, the Christians in the surrounding villages must be visited and cared for. Besides all *this,* the pastor has a field of from fifteen to twenty-five villages in which he must tour, carrying the Gospel into every street and bazaar and hamlet, becoming all things to all men that he may by all means save some. What a glorious opportunity! What a field for work! What skill, what tact, what intelligence, what gifts of leadership, what patience in adversity, what faith in God and love for men are called for in this great task! Here is the real training ground for the leaders of the Telugu people—not in the quiet and seclusion of the mission compound, but in the stress and strain of the village life. On this stern battle-field prophets of the Most High are born and ministers of God's grace are touched with a new power.

Theology on the Field

The missionary must be "jack of all trades." Evangelist, educationalist, industrialist, builder, accountant, mechanic, doctor, farmer—these are a few of the lines in which he must specialize. He must also have his theological seminary. The course in Ramapatnam Seminary is quickly over and the tendency thereafter is to pack away the books in a corner and grow stale. It is for the missionary to see that the books, especially the Bible, are not put away, and that the men keep fresh and alert, becoming workers that need not be ashamed, rightly dividing the word of truth. Hence the need of the summer school, where we can quietly meet with our men and, opening the windows of the soul to the light of heaven, can sit at the feet of the great Teacher. Here the missionary gathers his men about him and imparts unto them the deep things of God, as he has been taught by the Spirit of God. Minds are open and receptive, hearts are hungry to know the truth, human need cries out on every side in the unreached multitudes and the God of all grace is near at hand to speak and bless. What a meeting-place for God and man! What a Bethel even though it be in the *desert* or in the jungle!

Two weeks in September, when the rains are on, are devoted to our *Ashram* (retreat). From forty to fifty men (pastors of the churches, village school teachers and a sprinkling of Bible women) are in attendance. Courses of study are given in Christian Doctrine— "God," "Man," "Sin," "Christ," "The New Testament Church," "Life of Christ," "Parables of Jesus," "Sermon on the Mount," the "Apostle Paul" and many others. A course on "Old Testament Bible Stories" is perhaps the most popular of all. The men are taught the art of telling these wonderful stories to the people in their own language and drawing out the spiritual truths hidden therein. They realize as never before that the Bible is the most wonderful story-book in the world, perfectly adapted to the mind of a little child or to the intellect of the most learned man. With a little practice some of the preachers developed a real talent in the art of story telling, presenting them with vividness and imagination. Long afterwards, far out in the villages in the homes of the people, came echoes from our *Ashram*. Another course of vital interest to the men is the "Village School." Model lessons are given by the teachers and criticisms by the class. The problems and difficulties of the village school are threshed out in a lively manner and sometimes with considerable heat, and many helpful and constructive suggestions offered for the improvement and betterment of the school. From time to time the District Educational Officer and the head master of the government training school are called in to give instructive and stimulating lectures on the reconstruction of the village school. At the evening sessions lantern lectures are given on popular themes such as "The British Empire," "Religious Movements in India," "India's Social Needs," "Life of Christ," "Bunyan's *Pilgrim's Progress*" and others. The school closes with a farewell meeting of prayer, praise and worship in which opportunity is given to the men to testify to the spiritual benefit received during the days of study and meditation on the deep things of God.

Indian Leaders at the Helm

Early in our service on the Kurnool field, feeling the need of training our men and preparing them for larger responsibilities, we came to the conclusion that the most effective way was to give them work to do and let them learn by experience. Accordingly in 1905, instead of conducting our *nelasary* ourselves as formerly, we put them in charge. We had them elect their own officers, appoint their committees (the most important of which was the Reference Committee to which all requests were offered in consultation with the missionary) and transact all business. Subjects for papers were assigned a month in advance and a free hand was given to discussion which never failed to be

Dr. and Mrs. Stanton with Kurnool Indian leaders in Summer School, 1933.
Our "Boys," trained and educated in the field.

of a lively nature. Sermons were preached and criticised and a whole day was devoted to Bible study. In this way the monthly meeting became a training school for the men, teaching them to take responsibilities and greatly quickening them in spirit. Finally in 1909 a further step was taken and the Kurnool Gospel Extension Society was launched. Year by year new lines of work were taken up and larger responsibilities assumed, until at last the whole responsibility for the field work—evangelistic and education—was taken over by the Society. In view of these larger activities, at the November meeting in 1925 it was resolved to change the name of the Society to that of the Kurnool Field Association and to adopt a new constitution in line with these activities.

The Association meets once in two months and is a live, functioning body, doing definite work, carrying heavy responsibilities and working harmoniously and enthusiastically for the extension of the Kingdom within its borders. It has taken an immense burden off the hands of the missionary, has aroused new interest and enthusiasm in the work, has revealed new possibilities of leadership in the workers and has released new resources of spiritual power for the prosecution of the work. The two lines of work undertaken by the Association lie near to the hearts of the people and appeal powerfully to their deepest sentiments.

The real test, however, of any such organization must be financial. However excellent its constitution and however efficient its administration, if it is not financially responsible for the work it administers the most vital and essential factor in its constitution is lacking. We can well be proud of the financial showing of the Kurnool Field Association.

1931-33 was a real testing time. A wide-spread movement towards Christianity swept over the Kurnool field. More than fifteen hundred converts were received by baptism in three years. As fast as the people came they demanded teachers.

We were besieged with requests for workers. Every *nelasary* was a field-day—delegations from the villages calling for teachers and new workers offering themselves for the work. Sometimes we were frightened, not knowing whereunto this thing would grow. Then when we looked into the eager, hungry faces of the new converts, clamoring not for food, but for a teacher to break unto them the Bread of Life, we could not deny them. We dared not say "No" to the multitudes pressing into the Kingdom. As fast as God gave us the men, we thrust them out. In the first year of the revival thirty-one new workers were taken on by the Association; in the second year twenty-nine and in the third year, twenty—eighty new workers in three years! Our resources were taxed to the utmost. But we never said to any group of converts, "We have no men and we have no money." In a wonderful way God supplied our need. We never lacked the men and we never lacked the money. In the third year of the ingathering (1933) the Kurnool Field Association, carrying this great work, received and disbursed over fifteen thousand rupees—not one *pice* of which was mission money!

In these days of retrenchment, of diminishing appropriations, of depleted treasuries, of "cuts" and closures and retreats, it is with a thrill of delight that we realize that, in our Telugu Christians, poor though they may be, we have mighty resources for the Kingdom of God. Instead of closing stations, dismissing workers and abandoning fields, why not tap the hidden resources of the Telugu Christians? Instead of looking to an over-burdened Board and a dwindling denominational budget, why not look to the people of God among the Telugus? We have so long had our eyes fixed on the horses and chariots of Egypt that we have failed to see the swift moving of our God in the tops of the mulberry trees. Surely we need not cross the seas to find the resources of the Kingdom. They are here in the bazaars and streets of India, in the hearts and homes of the humble Telugu Christians no less than in the gilded palaces of the West!

Who are the Leaders

When the Layman's Commission visited India in 1931, they thought that we had no leaders in the Telugu Mission. They mistook the university graduate for the leader. We have our university graduates in the Telugu Mission, some fifty or more of them—head masters and teachers in our high schools, training schools and theological seminary and zealous and efficient workers in the mission at large. They include, Rev. Josiah Ramanjalu, Ramapatnam Theological Seminary; Rev. M. George, Head Master, Bapatla Training School; Rev. M. J. Prakashham, Adult Literacy Secretary; Rev. P. Ravi Varma, Manager Ongole High School; Rev. B. R. Moses, Promotional Secretary Telugu Baptist Convention; Miss Alice Veeraswamy, Head Mistress, Nellore Girls High School; Miss K. Chandravarty, Telugu Pundit, Woman's Christian College, Madras, and many others. We are proud of these men and women who have risen from the ranks of the outcastes to positions of high responsibility.

But we must not think that in a great mission now numbering 117,776 church members (1947 report) and representing a Christian community of 250,000, leadership is confined to university graduates. If we think for a moment of the background of this great movement in the Telugu Mission and seek to understand the mighty spiritual upheaval which has transformed these outcastes into a new people, we will not fail to discern the men of God who have led these people out of the darkness and bondage of heathenism into the glorious light and liberty of the children of God. Yerraguntla Pariah, one of the first converts of Dr. Clough, was a mighty man of God, but he was unlettered and untutoured and scarcely able to read his New Testament. The leaders in our Telugu Mission are the pastors of the Telugu churches, who have been raised from among the people and separated unto the Gospel of God—men who through the deep experience of life have come to know Christ in the fellowship of His sufferings and the sufferings of their people. They are not university graduates, but they are *leaders.* We have such men on the Kurnool field as pastors of our churches. These men are not only leading their churches into a higher life and evangelizing a score or more of villages within their church circle, but they are carrying the whole burden of the evangelistic and educational work of a great field three times the size of the state of Rhode Island with a population of half a million—and that without any financial aid from America! When we remember that these men are only three generations out of heathenism and, in some cases, only two, and that their forefathers were outcastes *Madigas* beating the drums before idol processions, we can only exclaim, "What hath God wrought!"

After Forty Years

As we look back over these forty years, we are thankful above all else that God permitted us to spend these years on the Kurnool field without change and without interruption. The little handful of Christians of those early days has grown to a great multitude of over six thousand church members, gathered into fifteen organized churches, self-governing and self-supporting. The little band of unlettered and untrained men who greeted us when we first came to Kurnool has grown to a splendid force of one hundred and fifty workers from among the boys and girls of this field, educated and trained in our own schools. These men and these women, who are now carrying the responsibilities of this great field, ministering to the flock of God, carrying the Gospel far and wide through all the villages, teaching the children in the schools, bearing the heat and burden of the day, as good soldiers of Jesus Christ—*these* are our "crown of rejoicing", our "epistle, known and read of all men." And these we shall never forget!

XIII

NEW LIFE IN AN OLD LAND: GOD AT WORK

"THE *Kingdom of God is as if a man should cast seed into the ground and the seed should spring up and grow, he knoweth not how . . . first the blade, then the ear, then the full corn in the ear.*"

The picture is true. The seed which is the word of God, is cast into human hearts. It springs up and grows, we know not how, from the tiny blade to the ripened corn. Human hands sow the seed, human hearts receive it; but the springing into life, the growth from stage to stage to a final end, is strange, hidden, mysterious. The visible agent is man, but the unseen worker is God. During all the years of our missionary life, we have sown the seed and while we "slept by night and watched by day," God has worked.

Just a Word

Touring to the east, on my way to Anandapuram I left the main road and struck off across the country on my good old horse, Rani. After going a short distance, I found myself in a dense forest and quite lost my way. After wandering about for some time, I came out finally into the open and in the distance was a village. As I drew up in front of a group of houses, the people came running out to see the white man on the horse. It was a wild place and doubtless they had never seen a white man before. Making a salaam, I said:

"What village is this?"

"Lingapuram," they replied.

"And who are you?" I asked, referring to their caste.

"We are *Madigas,*" they answered. Seeing their mud huts, their tattered garments and their disshevelled hair, I knew they had spoken the truth. "Don't you want to become Christians?" I asked with a smile. They looked at each other and laughed as though such a thing were an impossibility for *Madigas.* As it was rapidly getting dark, I inquired the way to Anandapuram and went on.

Early the next morning before I was awake, I heard some one calling:

"Ayya, Ayya" (Sir, Sir).

Stepping outside the little rest house where I was camped, I saw a motley throng of ten or fifteen men. They bowed low, as they saw me, making their salaams.

The leader stepped forward and said:

"Sir, you came to our village last night and spoke kindly to us and asked if we did not want to become Christians. Last night after you were gone we talked it over with our *peddalu.* We think this is a *manchi mattam* (good religion). We want to be baptized, for God brought you to our village."

As I looked into their earnest faces and heard their simple confession of faith, I was astonished and praised God. Not many days afterward we baptized these people in the waters of the old Kurnool-Cuddapah Canal that flows by their village. The whole *palem* had become Christian! And how did it happen? Just a word was spoken as we passed by! So near is the Kingdom!

The Lad who Dared to be Baptized

On the southern tour we pitched our tent at Uppalapad. Though we had been touring the Kurnool field for nearly forty years, we had never seen that village before. It was away up in the hills in a wild and inaccesible place. But though the missionary had never been there preacher Ramiah had been. The people heard his word with joy, threw away their idols and their toddy pots and were waiting for baptism. After the meeting in which we examined them for baptism, just as we were starting for the baptismal service, a young man came running to us in great excitement. When this young lad had asked his *Sudra* master for leave to be baptized, the man beat him with a big stick and told him to go back to his work. Then the outcaste lad boldly faced his *Sudra* master and said:

"Sir, you may beat me until the blood comes, but I shall be baptized this day."

And he came and this lad and twenty-two other men and women in that village boldly confessed their Lord in baptism that day in the presence of their *Sudra* masters! A new *"Acts of the Apostles"* is being written in India today! By the grace of God the despised outcaste has become a man! "And when they saw the boldness of Peter and John, they took knowledge of them that they had been with Jesus!"

The Joy of Finding Lost Sheep

On the western tour we set out one morning to reach a village fifteen miles away on the opposite bank of the Tungabadhra River. We went in the little old Ford as far as the river and there the pastor said he would have a pony to take us the remaining five miles to the village. But, alas, the pony was not forthcoming and there was nothing to do but to walk it! It was in the month of May, the hottest month in the year. The sun was beating down like a furnace. The sand in the river bed was deep and hot and the way was long. By the time I reached the village my throat was parched and dry. I was burning with the heat and quite exhausted.

But as soon as we entered the *palem* a half dozen big stalwart fellows of splendid physique came running to meet us, making low salaams and greeting us with smiles and many expressions of affection. In the joy of seeing them we quite forgot our thirst and the heat and the long walk in the burning sand. And as these strong, sturdy fellows stood up and confessed their faith in Christ, it seemed as if we drank anew of that living water whereof if a man drink he shall never thirst again. We walked ten miles that day through the burning sand under a tropical sun, but in our joy we forgot all that. For were not nineteen men born anew into the Kingdom of God in Demada village that day?

The God in the Corn-Field

Agraharam Job was an old man, eighty years of age, venerable in appearance, with a mark of distinction unusual in a *Madiga*. His Hindu name was Nagappa, but we called him Job because he had suffered much. His village was Agraharam in the Pattikonda Taluk some sixty miles from Kurnool. Though an outcaste *Madiga,* he was a rich man. *Madigas* are called the "slaves of the soil", for they till the fields and do the menial work for the *Sudra* masters. Very few of them have lands of their own. But Job had six yoke of oxen, a half dozen servants and one hundred and fifty acres of the finest black-cotton land in the district. His house was as large as a church. It had to be, for he had a huge family—five sons and five daughters-in-law and their children—all living together as a joint family in one big house. And under the same roof he kept his oxen and cattle and buffaloes, his goats and his chickens. No Hindu would think of keeping his cattle anywhere else!

Now Job was a very devout old man—what the Hindus call a *bhakta* (devotee). Out in his fields he had built a little shrine to the goddess Gurkhamma, a local deity in those parts. Every day he would go to the shrine and worship Gurkhamma, making an offering of rice and cocoanut and decking the idol with a garland of flowers. For many years the old man had done this—worshipping God as best he knew out in his field, in the midst of the growing corn, under the open sky! How deep the devotion of the Hindu heart! How passionate the longing for *shanthi* (peace)! But one day when the old man went to the shrine, a strange feeling came over him. He could not kneel. He had no desire to worship. The offering he brought for Gurkhamma fell from his hands. The flowers seemed to wither. What if Gurkhamma was only a stick or a stone! Can she make the corn to ripen? Can she feed my cattle, my sons and my daughters? Can she bring peace to my heart?

Greatly disturbed and agitated, he went to preacher Ramiah.

"Sir, my Gurkhamma is dead," he cried in despair. "This morning I could not kneel at her shrine. My flowers withered. My offering fell from my hand. I could not speak. My Gurkhamma is dead! To what god shall I go?"

"There is but one God," said Ramiah, "the Almighty, maker of heaven and earth, Father of all mankind and of His Son, the Lord Jesus Christ who came to save sinners."

"Is that true?" the old man eagerly asked.

"Yes, it is true," Ramiah said. "Believe in Him and you shall be saved.

"I believe," he cried. "Save me, Blessed Christ."

A strange peace came into the old man's heart and his face shone with a new joy.

After this blessed experience, he began to persuade the other members of his family, that they too might find Christ. But his daughters-in-law were obstinate and would have nothing to do with this new religion. He called in his

Christian friends and preacher Ramiah to talk with them. At last they were won over. Christmas day was a day of great rejoicing in that house. For on that day Agraharam Job and his wife and five sons and their wives were baptized! As the old man came up out of the baptismal waters he bowed himself and worshipped God! "The Lord, He is God," he cried, "and besides Him there is none else!"

Revival at Jupad-Bannur

Jupad-Bannur on the Kurnool-Cuddapa Canal was one of the bright spots on the Kurnool field. We were very proud of the village. Some fifty of the outcaste Madigas had become Christians. They had a prosperous school with forty bright and eager little children in attendance, taught by one of our most capable teachers and his wife. A half dozen *Sudra* boys also were attending the school in spite of the rigid rules of caste. The Christians' houses were neat and clean. They had given up drinking though toddy was plentiful in their village which was famous for its date-palm trees from which the toddy is drawn. Every night and on Sundays they met for prayers in their little chapel and worshipped God with songs of praise and thanksgiving.

For many days they enjoyed this happy life in the new religion. But one day the old Tempter came, sowing discord among them. Trouble arose. They were split into factions over a senseless dispute. Not being able to settle it among themselves, they went to the courts to fight it out. Litigation is one of the curses of the Hindus. Immersed in this conflict, they lost all interest in their religion. Only two or three attended prayers. The school dwindled and finally had to be closed. The situation seemed hopeless. After several months of wandering in this waste, squandering all their money in the courts, they came to me and confessed their fault and said that God had given them a new mind. They wanted to come back and start anew. Would I send them a teacher? "Certainly", I said. "You shall have a teacher if you want one." A new man was sent. They rallied about him. The opposing parties were reconciled. Christians and heathen all joined in prayers. A new school was erected in place of the old tumble-down hut. The children flocked to the school once more. On a Sunday when I camped in the village, the people welcomed me with garlands and gifts of rice and sweets. The little schoolhouse was packed to the doors with an eager throng of worshippers, praising God for the great things He had done for them. After the morning service we baptized nineteen happy converts in the waters of the old Kurnool-Cuddapa Canal. The whole *palem* had been lifted to a new life. They were in the midst of revival!

Return of the Prodigal

Some twenty-five years ago the *Madigas* of Bollavaram became Christians. For a time the work went on well. They had a nice little school. The schoolhouse they built themselves and they were very proud of it. They were Christians now—no longer despised *Madigas!* Then like a bolt out of the sky, a very sad and shocking thing happened. Their teacher proved false, betrayed them and ran away! Left without a teacher, all of them relapsed into heathenism. Rarely do our Christians revert to heathenism. But in this case they did. They grew the *juttu*—the tuft of hair on the top of the head which every Hindu wears. They put on the marks of Hinduism. They took to the toddy pot—the curse of the outcaste. They ate the meat of dead animals, like vultures. They beat the tom-toms in heathen processions and slaughtered buffaloes at the shrine of heathen gods. For twenty-five years they wandered in the wilderness of heathenism.

But God is great. His mercy endureth forever. One day a deputation came to me from that village. I was astonished to see them. What did they want? They said they were tired of the old heathen life. Like the prodigal of old, they had been feeding on the husks the swine did eat. They wanted to come back to the Father's house. Would we take them back? They were very much in earnest. As I looked into the faces of these men and saw the unsatisfied hunger of their hearts, I was deeply moved. I told them to come to the next *nelasary*. At the appointed time they came—thirty men and women—confessed their sins and were received back into the church. With joy we welcomed them from the "far country," home at last.

The Christian Sannyasi

His name was Tellari Sunkiah. Though an outcaste *Madiga,* he was highly respected by the village *Reddi* and the caste people, for he was faithful in the discharge of his duties as village watchman and was thoroughly honest. The *Madigas* in Brahmankotkur, his village, had long since become Christians. There was a prosperous mission school in the *palem,* taught by a Christian teacher, and the pastor from Gadidamudagu regularly visited the village and conducted prayers. But for some reason Sunkiah did not join. When approached he would say:

"Yes, I am believing," but he did not come.

Time went on. Many years passed. He became an old man. Finally one day he came to the pastor and said:

"Sir, I want to be baptized. I am an old man now. This is a *maya lokham* (world of illusion). When I die, I want to go home."

With joy we baptized him and received him into the little church.

After he was baptized, one day he went to the village *Reddi* and said:

"Sir, I am a Christian now. I have found the true God and I want to give up my work as *tellari* (village watchman) and go about the villages and tell the people about God."

The *Reddi* was astonished to hear a Madiga outcaste talk about God, but he had a deep respect for the old man and he said:

"Go and tell the people about your God."

So Sunkiah became a Christian *sannyasi,* only he did not put on the yellow robe of the *sannyasi.* But taking his bamboo staff in his hand, he went from village to village telling the people about God. And what do you suppose this old village watchman had to say about God? All his life he had bowed down to dumb idols. He had worshipped Maramma, Sunkalamma and Polaramma, the village gods of cholera, smallpox and all the rest, but what did he know about the true God? He had never studied in the schools and no one had ever taught him anything. Well, the old man had a great text. No one ever knew where he got it or who taught him. But as he went from village to village, wherever he went, he repeated the words of that text in Telugu: *"Devadu manchi vadu; Devadu premagalla vadu."* ("God is good; God is Love."

That was his text and that was his sermon. As he walked along the road, as he sat in the market-place, as he went from house to house, to every man he met, he said: "God is good; God is Love."

In some mysterious way, untaught and unlettered, this old man had seized upon the deepest and profoundest truth of the Christian religion and was telling it to everbody. "Flesh and blood" had not revealed it unto him, but his heavenly Father. God taught him. And at last, as the old man was dying, he beckoned to his friends about him and whispered, "God is good; God is Love."

Swept by Fire

While we were on tour news came that the Regadagudur Christian *palem* had been burnt down by fire, this being the third time in three years that this calamity had befallen them. The houses of the poor people in the Kurnool district are built with mud walls and roofs of bamboo and thatch. If a fire is once started among the houses, nothing but a miracle can save them. The Christians of Regadagudur had been planning a Harvest Festival for which great preparations had been made. When the news came to us in camp of this great calamity, I thought that all was over. But the people, nothing daunted, sent word that the Harvest Festival would be held as usual and that we must come without fail.

When we reached the village, I found every house in the *palem* burnt to the ground, the people exposed to the sun and the heat and everything in ruins. In a half-hour's time everything had been swept away. I expected to find the chapel in the same condition, but God graciously spared the little chapel. In front of the chapel was a beautiful *jevee* tree with wide-spreading branches, providing delightful shade in the hot season, but that also was now only a burnt and charred stump. But, thank God, the chapel was untouched! It seemed a miracle. And what was our surprise to find the chapel beautifully decorated with garlands of flowers and festoons of coloured paper, decked out in the most festive manner. Here indeed was a revelation of the faith and courage of this devoted people in the midst of the ruin and devastation wrought by the fire. Not only this, in the services on Sunday that followed, there was a wonderful spirit of devotion and joy without one word of complaint. And at the night meeting when the Harvest Festival offerings were taken, the people gave with wonderful abandon—the total offering amounting to Rs 110. A wonderful offering of God's people such as we had never seen before. That night in the little chapel we had a thanksgiving service, praising God who had made His people "willing in the day of His power." Thank-offerings in a fire-swept village!

Flowers on her Grave

She was a Bible woman in Gudur, a large and important village on the Kurnool field. Her name was Chencamma. Every day she would go to the village to speak to the Hindu women about Jesus. Though she was an outcaste by birth, she had been educated and trained in the mission boarding school and she had an atractive and winsome personality. Wherever she went she made friends and the caste women of Gudur, both *Sudras* and *Brahmans,* welcomed her to their homes. They loved to hear her tell the Bible stories, so different from the stories of their Hindu gods and goddesses. Above all they loved the story of Jesus, the story of the Babe in the Manger and the Saviour on the Cross. They loved the beautiful Telugu songs, especially one, *"Yesu, ne nama mrutham—ma kento ruchi ayya"* ("Jesus, How sweet Thy Name to Me"). She would have to sing it over and over again to them and they would never tire. Her heart went out to these Hindu women and she longed for the day to come when they too would give their hearts to Jesus and find peace and pardon in Him.

In her visits to these Hindu homes she always did one thing. Before she left the home she would always ask permission to offer prayer. Her prayers were quite wonderful, so tender and touching. She seemed to be just talking to God, as indeed she was. Hindu women are very devout, but they had never heard anything like this. Chencamma's God seemed so near and so real! So day by day this humble Christian woman went about sowing the good seed of the Kingdom and letting her light shine in many a dark place.

Then one day a dark cloud swept over the village. Cholera broke out—the most dreaded and fearful of all plagues in India! As the epidemic swept on day by day, taking its fearful toll of human life, the people became panic-stricken. The nights were made hideous with wild scenes and cries of men and women, supposed to be possessed with the god. And finally the whole village joined in a *pedda devara* (great sacrifice) in which buffaloes and goats by the hundred were slaughtered before the shrine of Maramma in a vain effort to appease the angry goddess!

During those terrible days Chencamma was calm and unafraid. Like a ministering angel she went from house to house, nursing the sick, caring for the dying, comforting the bereaved. Finally she herself fell a victim to the dread disease. Surrounded by her sorrowing family and the little band of Christians to whom she had ministered so devotedly in her lifetime, she quietly slipped away and was at rest in the presence of her Lord. So great is the fear of cholera among the Hindus that no one dares even to touch the corpse and often men flee from its very presence. But when Chencamma died, the whole village turned out and laid flowers on her grave! So great was the love of this woman!

Truly, God is at work in this land. Everywhere the seed is springing up and bearing fruit. Everywhere God is stretching forth His hand to save. Harvest time has come.

"Say not ye, There are yet four months and then cometh the harvest. Behold, I say unto you, Lift up your eyes and look on the fields, for they are white already unto harvest."

XIV

THE HINDU HOME: A LITTLE CHILD SHALL LEAD THEM

THE home is the citadel of Hinduism. Dedicated by solemn rite and immemorial custom to the wife and mother, secluded from contact with the outside world and jealously guarded by the relentless hand of caste and the stern sanctions of religion, the home is the sacred shrine of Hinduism. Only the inmates and the closest friends may enter here. The outside world is banished. This inner sanctuary, with its doors barred and bolted by the frail hands of wives and mothers, we must besiege and take if ever we are to win India to Christ. The violent cannot take it by force, neither can the proud and the haughty prevail against it. In the name of Him who was "meek and lowly in heart" we must come as friend and helper, as brother and sister. Love will unlock the door.

Let us, then, take a look into this Hindu home and see what it is like. We are thinking now of a *Brahman* or high caste home. The joint-family system is observed in all Hindu homes. Parents, grand-parents, sons, daughters, daughters-in-law and children—all live under one roof and constitute one big family. Sons when married do not go away and form their own home, but remain as members of the paternal family. The father is revered as the head of the family and his authority is never questioned. The mother, if she has many sons and daughters, is honored and tenderly loved by her children. Among the Hindus "*Talli*" is a sacred name.

As the poet Tukeram says, the little Hindu bride goes out

from her mother's house "with dragging feet," wistfully looking behind. She is a mere child of twelve, or even younger, it may be. She has never seen her husband. Her parents and the elders have arranged the marriage. She had no choice. We of the West would not think such a marriage could possibly be a happy one. But strange as it may seem to us, the little child becomes a devoted wife and mother. From childhood she has heard from her mother's lips the appealing story of Sita, the faithful, the devoted, the spotless wife of Rama, as told in the immortal words of the *Ramayana,* and Sita has become to her an ideal, a guiding star. Her husband she reveres as lord and master. When he eats, she must stand and serve. When she accompanies him on the public road, she must walk behind him, never by his side. And when he dies, she becomes a widow for life and, in bitterness of soul, would fain mount the funeral pyre and perish in the flames.

With a devotion impossible for us of the West to understand, she clings to her idols, garlands them with flowers morning by morning, and worships at the shrine of her gods. She is punctillious in the observance of all the rites and ceremonies of her religion. She makes long pilgrimages to sacred places, worships at countless shrines, bathes in the waters of sacred rivers and offers the very hair of her head in vows to her god. Religion is the life of the Hindu woman. Sadhu Sundar Singh tells us how his mother was accustomed to rise early in the morning before dawn and for hours she would read the *Baghavadgita,* the Bible of the Hindus. From his earliest childhood she taught him the Hindu sacred Scriptures and impressed upon him the principles and duties of religion. Would that American mothers were as devoted!

Though there is much in this Hindu home, as we have seen, that is beautiful and appealing, there are many sad things too. Even in the name of the religion to which she so fondly clings, the Hindu woman suffers many cruel wrongs. The

Dharma Sastras says: "Day and night must women be kept in dependence by the male members of the family; they are never fit for independence; they are as impure as falsehood itself." And again: "Let a woman be in subjection to her father in her childhood, to her husband in her youth, to her sons in old age when her husband is dead; let a woman never enjoy independence." And they say: "If a woman's husband dies, let her live a life of chastity or else mount his funeral pyre"—an injunction from which arose the cruel custom of widow burning or *sati*. These are stern doctrines, consigning the Hindu woman to the place of a mere chattel in the hands of man. In Hinduism, as set forth in the *Dharma Sastras,* the lot of woman is a life of subjection, ending in days gone by in the flames of the funeral pyre. However, it must be said, in fairness, that the Hindus are, in many respects, better than their *Dharma Sastras.*

The joint-family system, while possessing many advantages as regards economy and while strengthening the bond of the family tie, almost inevitably lends itself to friction and strife among the members, especially the female members. The mother-in-law rules her daughters-in-law with a rod of iron and their lot is a very unhappy one. Proverbially daughters-in-law occupy a difficult position, even in western lands. But the little Hindu daughter-in-law, under the roof of her mother-in-law with no possibility of escape, occupies the most difficult one of all.

The Hindu wife, if she is blessed with sons and daughters to present to her noble lord, is happy indeed. But if she is childless—the greatest of all tragedies to befall a Hindu wife—a sad fate awaits her. In all probabality her noble lord will take another wife to rear him sons and daughters, for in such cases polygamy has the sanction of Hindu law.

Ramabai, the Child-Widow

The saddest thing in this Hindu home is the little child-widow. Married at twelve, or even younger, if her husband dies (even while she is still a child) she becomes a widow for life, with the curses of men and of gods resting on her innocent head.

I shall never forget little Ramabai. She came to our caste girls' school when she was a tiny little thing, hardly able to talk, for in India mothers often send their children to school to be free from the trouble of caring for them in the home. She was a *Brahman* girl of the highest caste with large sparkling eyes, beautiful black hair and a very sweet face. We soon came to love her dearly, she was so bright, intelligent and winsome. Quickly she learned to sing our beautiful Telugu songs and to pray to Jesus. She made rapid progress in her studies, for she was a remarkably intelligent child and each year she was promoted to a higher grade. With eager eyes and great joy we watched her development, as her mind unfolded to the new knowledge and her heart responded to the beautiful story of Jesus. Finally she reached her twelfth birthday and we knew that she could not come to school much longer, for according to the *Braham* custom she must soon be married. How our hearts ached for the dear child, so young, so innocent, so soon to be deprived of the happy school days and the sweet songs she loved so much and to be shut up in the prison-house of an Indian *Zenana!*

One day when I went to school and looked over the eager faces, I missed little Ramabai.

"Where is Ramabai?" I asked.

"Oh, she is gone," said the head mistress. "Her parents took her out of the school a month ago and last week she was married."

My heart sank within me as I heard the sad news. I could

not be reconciled to it. As soon as possible I went to see her father who was a high government official, a very fine man. As soon as I saw him I realized that something serious had happened. He was deeply agitated. Divining the cause, I said to him:

"I was at school the other day and missed little Ramabai. Shall we not see her any more? She was such a beautiful child and so fond of the school."

"Ah," said he sadly, "you know we *Brahmans* are slaves to our customs. All our education and enlightenment are in vain when it comes to things in the home. Here we are powerless and must submit. Ramabai was twelve years old and according to the practice of the *Brahmans* she must be married. All my women-folk demanded it and I dared not resist. However advanced and liberal-minded a Hindu may be in public, in the home he bows without question to the authority and dictates of the women of the house. So we had her married."

"Now that she is married," I said, "let us hope that the dear child will be happy."

"Happy, did you say? Ah," said he, "a terrible thing has happened. Two days after her marriage her husband died. The curse of the gods is upon her. Would that she had perished in the flames of the funeral pyre!"

Just as he spoke, the figure of a child darted across the inner court of the house, like a frightened bird, and passed out of sight. It was none other than little Ramabai, but oh so changed! Her beautiful hair which was like a crown of glory was gone. Her head was closely shaven. Her jewels of gold and precious stones with which she had always been adorned, her bracelets and anklets and necklace and ornaments for her hair—all had been stripped from her. Her face was smeared with ashes and she was clad in the coarse yellow garments of the Hindu widow. And what was the

Top: Mrs. Stanton with her big family of eighty bright and happy Hindu girls. Bottom: The girls doing *Kolattam* with music and song.

cause of all this? What had this poor little innocent thing done? "Innocent," did you say? Why, in a former birth she committed an unspeakable sin and this is her punishment. She is the cause of her husband's death. She is accursed of gods and hated of men! So say the sacred books of the Hindus. There are thousands of these little child-widows in India today and their cry is the cry of desolation and despair.

Our Caste Girls' School

Into this Hindu home in which there is so much that is beautiful and appealing, and yet so much of sadness and cruel wrong, how shall we seek entrance? How shall we win this home for Christ? One avenue of approach, and perhaps the best of all, is through the child. In Kurnool, in the heart of the town, under the shadow of the old *Nawab's* palace and leaning hard against an old Mohammedan mosque, is our caste girls' school under the management, in our day, of Mrs. Stanton—a door of hope and opportunity to the bright and attractive little Hindu girls who throng its doors. The school is one of the oldest institutions in the town, having been opened by our predecessors, the Thomssens, in 1891. The head mistress in our day was O. Visranthamma and all the teachers were our own Christian women who gave themselves with rare devotion to the teaching and training of these little ones. In the early days we had a Hindu head master. We thought it would be impossible to conduct a school for *Brahman* and high caste Hindu girls with Christian teachers. But we did not like the arrangement. The Hindu head master, with the marks of his religion emblazoned on his forehead, seemed to cancel out the Bible we were teaching and the religion we were preaching. Finally we decided at all costs to dispense with him. A Christian head mistress was appointed and a staff of Christian teachers. Much to our surprise and a rebuke to our feeble faith, not a girl left the school. The head mistress took hold of the work with enthusiasm, increased the strength of the school and in a very short time won the respect and esteem of all the parents. This was the more surprising from the fact that all of our Christian teachers were of *Madiga* extraction. An outcaste woman teaching a *Braham* child was something unheard of in this land of caste. But a miracle had happened. These women had been lifted from their low estate by the power of Christ and changed. The *Madiga* woman had become a *Brahman* in character and spirit. And the little girl who sat at her feet and looked upon her as a mother never thought of her as an outcaste. So wonderful is the transforming power of Christ!

Here in this school are a hundred or more Brahman and high caste girls. I wish you could see their bright little faces. Unlike the low castes they are very fair, with olive complexions, sparkling black eyes, regular features and black hair neatly done in braids. Decked in her beautiful Indian *sari* and gay jacket, loaded with jewels (the Hindu woman loves her jewels), with ear-rings, nose-rings, necklace, broaches, ornaments for the hair, bracelets (all of gold and precious stones) silver anklets and a silver belt about the waist and flowers in her hair, the little *Brahman* girl presents a charming and fascinating picture. On gala days especially the school is a veritable garden of flowers.

The girls are taught sewing, fancy work and music in addition to the regular lessons of the curriculum. It is a delight to see how interested they are in their work. They become expert with the needle and make beautiful doilies, handkerchiefs, table-spreads, scarfs and exquisite lace work and embroidery. Hindus are extremely fond of music and to sing and play is considered a fine accomplishment. A Hindu music teacher is employed in the school who teaches the girls to play the little hand-harmonium and to sing the beautiful

Telugu songs to Indian music. Marching and drill and the Indian *kolattam,* which is much like our May Pole (done to the accompaniment of music and singing) are great favorites of which the girls never tire. English is taught in the fifth and sixth standards. Even Hindu girls are eager to learn the language of the English and many of them outstrip their brothers. They do not get far along in our little school, but they are able to read simple English and to recite English poetry and even sing English songs. Many a girl from our little school has gone on to high school and college and taken her place among the new women of India. On the occasion of the deputation visit of Dr. J. C. Robbins, our Foreign Secretary from America, in the public meeting given in his honor, our little caste girls presented Shakespeare's *Merchant of Venice* and the little Brahman girl who took the leading part astonished the audience with her acting and the fluency of her English.

Daily the school opens with the singing of one of our beautiful Telugu songs and with prayer. It is an impressive sight when these little Hindu girls reverently bow their heads and repeat the Lord's Prayer. The heart of the little child instinctively turns to God. The sixth standard is the highest, for that is as long as we can keep the girls in the school. Then the little Hindu girl must return to the seclusion of her home and the bright happy days of childhood are over. But we have the assurance that she takes with her the priceless treasure of Jesus' love. During the days spent in the school she has eagerly learned the most beautiful story in all the world and her tender heart has responded to its moving appeal. She had learned to sing many heart-searching Telugu songs. She has learned to pray to Jesus and we know that the good seed of the Kingdom planted in her young heart will spring up and bear fruit in God's appointed time. In the quiet hours in her home she sings the songs over and over again. The sweet story of Jesus which she learned in school she tells to her mother and sisters and brothers. And often she lifts her heart in prayer to the loving Father about whom she has heard. She is a witness in the home. The light is shining in the darkness and the darkness cannot put it out. "A little child shall lead them."

It is the custom of the school to give an annual prize distribution at the close of the school year. It is a great occasion. The mothers of the girls and many of the leading women of the town are present. The girls are decked out in their many-coloured *saris* and their finest jewels. On one of these occasions the girls acted the Biblical Drama of *Shadrach, Meshach* and *Abednego*. With wonderful spirit and fervor they depicted the story of the King, the Golden Image, the Firey Furnace and the three Saints who refused to bow down to the Image. The Hindu women present, many of them the mothers of the girls, were deeply affected by the recital and the lesson went home to their hearts. Who shall say that these girls will not one day take their stand in reality in their own homes, refusing to bow down to the dumb idols of their fathers!

On another occasion one of the brightest girls in the sixth standard, a Brahman girl and a very remarkable child, requested that she be given a Bible instead of a doll and so on the appointed day she stepped up very proudly before the whole school and the assembled mothers and took her treasured prize. Shall we not pray that this Bible may be the means of bringing not only this child but her whole family to the feet of Him of whom it speaks?

This little caste girls' school in the town, established over fifty years ago, still keeps on its quiet and peaceful way. In the midst of all vicissitudes and changes it stands unmoved. It seems to have drunk of the fountain of eternal youth and keeps ever green. The devoted band of women who work there year after year with little remuneration minister to the little ones who are placed in their care with a love and tenderness like that of their Master. The fruit of what they do is not seen and never will be seen in this world, but they care not, for the harvest is with God. It is theirs to sow the seed in tender hearts, to water it with their tears and their prayers and to see by faith the invisible and the eternal.

XV

MAHATMA GANDHI: CRUSADER AND SAINT

INDIA has given birth to many illustrious sons—warriors, statesmen, poets, philosophers, saints. One of the greatest of these was Mahatma Gandhi, the Indian patriot, mystic and saint. What shall we think of this frail little man in a loin cloth, living in a mud hut in a tiny village, far removed from the haunts of civilization, subsisting on dates and nuts and goat's milk, smilingly plying his spinning wheel and weaving the threads that bind the hearts of millions of his countrymen in an indissoluble bond, prophet of *satyagraha* (non-violence), arousing his people not by the sword but by the power of "soul-force" to a mighty struggle for freedom, often cast into prison by the strong hand of the British *Raj* whose power he defied, fasting well-nigh unto death in times of great crisis, hated and feared by some, loved and revered by millions. Some called him demagogue, dictator, *sabateur;* millions worshipped him as *Rishi* (Saint). Incredible man! What shall we think of him? Where shall we place him?

In June, 1942, Louis Fischer, author and correspondent, spent a week with Gandhi in Sevagram, the village where Gandhi lived. In *A Week With Gandhi* (Duell, Sloan, and Pierce) he says: "My talks with Gandhi were a rich and stimulating experience. Lord Linlithgow, the Viceroy at Delhi, said to me: 'Gandhi is the biggest thing in India.' "

Marshal Jan Christian Smuts, Gandhi's old antoganist in South Africa, recently paid this tribute to him: "Gandhi is one of the great men of the Asiatic world. He is a great patriot, a great man and a great spiritual leader." John Gunther,

PHOTO BY UNDERWOOD AND UNDERWOOD

Mahatma Gandhi—crusader and saint. Some called him demagogue, dictator, *sabateur*: millions worshiped him as *Rishi*, Saint, Mahatma.

author of *Inside Asia,* in a brilliant characterization of Gandhi calls him "an incredible combination of Jesus Christ, Tammany Hall and your father . . . the greatest Indian since Buddha."[1]

Gandhi's Religion

Whatever we may think of Gandhi, one thing we can confidently affirm. Gandhi was a profoundly religious man. Though he did not call himself a Christian he was very deeply influenced by Christianity. John Gunther says, "Gandhi is probably more like Christ than any man in the political sphere who has ever lived."[2] Some years ago Gandhi is reported to have said: "The man to whom I owe most, the man to whom India owes most, is the man who has never set foot in India and that man is Christ."

In his early career in South Africa Gandhi made friends with some Christian people, both Dutch and English, and had happy intercourse with them. Through their persuasion he read through the whole Bible and came to see the greatness of Christ's moral teaching in the Sermon on the Mount. His study at this time led him to think seriously of accepting Christianity. At a later date he writes: "I have endeavoured to study the Bible. I consider it a part of my Scriptures. I am not a biased Hindu, but a humble and impartial student of religion with a great leaning towards Christianity."

How profoundly Gandhi was influenced by Christianity can be seen from the following quotations from his writings:

> "Faith that transends reason is our only Rock of Ages."
>
> "God chooses as His instruments the humblest and weakest of His creatures to fulfill Himself."
>
> "Only in God's strength are we strong. And only those who cast their cares and fears on that Immeasurable Power have faith in God." (Harijan, June 3, 1939.)

[1] John Gunther, **Inside Asia,** p. 344. Harper and Brothers
[2] Ibid, p. 367.

"But who am I? I have no strength save what God gives me. I have no authority over my countrymen save the purely moral. If He holds me to be a fit instrument for the spread of non-violence in place of the awful violence now ruling the world, He will give me the strength and show me the way. My greatest weapon is mute prayer. The cause of peace is in God's good hands. Nothing can happen but by His will expressed in His eternal, changeless Law which is **He.** We neither know Him nor His Law, save through the glass darkly. But the faint glimpse of the Law is sufficient to fill me with joy, hope and faith in the future." (Harijan, December 9, 1939.)

Gandhi's creed, if we may so characterize it, is expressed in the following illuminating statement:

"I do perceive that, whilst everything around me is ever-changing and ever-dying, there is, underlying that change, a living Power that is changeless, that holds all together, that creates, dissolves and re-creates. That informing Power and Spirit is God . . . . I see it as purely benevolent, for I can see that in the midst of death, life persists; in the midst of untruth, truth persists; in the midst of darkness, light persists. Hence I gather that God is life, truth and light. He is Love. He is the Supreme Good."[1]

These are the words and sentiments of a Christian and not of a Hindu. Surely the Master would say to such a sincere soul: "Thou art not far from the Kingdom."

In his religious life Gandhi layed great stress on prayer. "I can, and often have, done without food for days on end," he says, "but I could not do without prayer even for a single day." He rose daily at 4:30 for morning prayers. Evening prayers were more formal. All of the members of the *Ashram,* men and women, (about seventy) were present. Verses from the *Koran,* the *Bhagavadgita* and the Bible were recited. Prayers were offered. Sometimes Gandhi sat in perfect silence during the whole service. Monday was his "Day of Silence" which was given up to prayer and meditation. On this day

[1] Columbia Gramophone Record, quoted by John Gunther in **Inside Asia,** p. 367—Harper and Brothers.

he would do no work, however urgent the call might be. No important work was undertaken without prayer for God's guidance. Before his last great fast he said, "I am praying for light and guidance without which there will be no fast."

In Gandhi's little one-room cottage at Sevagram there was only one decoration on the bare walls. It was a picture of Christ on the Cross and underneath is the inscription, *"He is our Peace."* His favorite hymn was "When I survey the Wondrous Cross." When he completed his twenty-one days' fast, prayers were offered and he asked that his favorite hymn be sung. These little incidents reveal better than anything else, perhaps, his deep reverance for Christ.

Gandhi—Friend of Man

Gandhi was a great friend of man. "I claim to be the greatest democrat of modern times," he recently said. "I have faith in human nature." All men of whatever race or clan he claimed as his brothers. He loved all men—even Englishmen. "I have no hate in me for a single Englishman," he said. "I am not interested in driving the Englishman out of India. I am interested in converting him into a servant of India. I feel toward him precisely as I feel toward an Indian, no matter what his faith may be." The warm friendship that sprang up between Gandhi and Lord Halifax when the latter was viceroy of India is well known. That friendship tided India over a very difficult period in her history.

When Gandhi was interned in the Aga Khan's palace at Poona in 1942, he carried on a remarkable correspondence with Viscount Wavell, the Viceroy. Addressing this powerful ruler of four hundred million people as "Dear Friend," he wrote:

> I am looked upon by representatives of the British Government as the greatest enemy of the British. Since I regard myself as a

> friend and servant of humanity, including the British, in token of my good will, I call you, foremost representative of the British in India, 'My Friend'.

Viscount Wavell, replying just after Mrs. Gandhi's death, wrote as follows:

> Dear Mr. Gandhi: I take this opportunity to express to you deep sympathy from my wife and myself at the death of Mrs. Gandhi. We understand what this loss must mean to you after so many years of companionship.

It is not often that correspondence between a viceroy of India and a *Mahatma* in prison is conducted on such a high plane as this.

Strange to say this odd little man had a charm all of his own and a keen sense of humor. He made friends wherever he went, and among all classes of people. When in London at the Round Table Conference, he met Charlie Chaplin and had a delightful half hour's visit with him. During his imprisonment in 1924 he had a serious attack of appendicitis which nearly cost him his life. Though he denounced Western medicine as "black magic" and would have nothing to do with it, he was operated upon by a skillful English surgeon and tenderly cared for by English nurses. As if to repay them, during the long days of his convalescence he laughed and joked with them and made himself so agreeable that he completely won the heart of the surgeon general and the nurses and they were very sorry when the time came for the little man to leave the hospital.

When Lord Reading was leaving England to take up his duties as viceroy of India, so the story goes, Sir Samuel Hoare, Secretary of State for India, warned him not to see Gandhi lest he be captivated by his charm! A dangerous man was this Mahatma!

With his famous toothless smile, his large brown eyes and his affable manner, Gandhi had a most fascinating personality.

His jailors have all been on excellent terms with him and the police always handled him with great deference. Even in the inner recesses of the government he was affectionately referred to as "the old gentleman." Frederick William Wilson, Editor of the *Bombay Times,* who knew him well, says: "I do not think I have met a single Englishman, whether official or otherwise, who, having met Gandhi, has not succumbed to his charm."

But Gandhi was the friend not only of the high and mighty, but of the meek and lowly. Himself a high caste Hindu, born and reared in a caste-ridden land, he renounced caste and admitted to his *Ashram* without distinction men and women of all castes– *Brahmans, Sudras,* Europeans, outcastes. He came out boldly and fearlessly as the champion of the outcastes whom he calls *Harijans* (Children of God). He admitted them to his *Ashram,* lived in a little village surrounded by them and even adopted an outcaste child as a member of his family. Not only this, Gandhi went all over India preaching against "untouchability", as he called it, seeking to remove the social, political and religious disabilities under which the untouchable has so long and so cruelly suffered at the hands of his Hindu master. Gandhi made the removal of "untouchability" one of the fundamental tenets of the Indian National Congress of which he was the leader. "I would rather that Hinduism die, than that untouchability should live," he affirmed. "The very idea of high and low among Hindus must be rooted out," he declared. He told his fellow-Hindus that the untouchable is his brother and just as truly a man in the sight of God as he himself. It was a revolutionary doctrine for India, shaking Hinduism to its foundations.

The Struggle for Freedom

Gandhi's greatest contribution to India and to the world,

perhaps, is his doctrine of non-violence. He says that he first found this principle in Christ's teaching in the Sermon on the Mount. "Resist not evil." "Love your enemies and pray for them that despitefully use you." Unlike some of us, he took Jesus quite literally and at once accepted non-violence as the rule of his life. For this concept he has two words. The first was *satyagraha,* which means literally "truth-force," or as he called it "soul-force"—a spiritual weapon, the power of truth and love, instead of violence and hate. Violence he believed wrong. Evil is to be met and overcome, not by violence, but by "soul-force." The other word was *ahimsa* (harmlessness) doing no injury to anyone. The *satyagrahi* (disciple of non-violence) must harbor no anger or resentment; must never retaliate; must submit to arrest, if need be; must love his enemy. "To bear all kinds of torture without murmer or resentment" was Gandhi's creed. This doctrine of non-violence was an intimate part of Gandhi's religion. "It is," he said, "a purely religious instrument and its use, therefore, is possible only in men religiously inclined." "My faith is built on non-violence," he affirmed. "For me there is no laying down arms."

With great astuteness Gandhi made the *charka* (spinning wheel) the symbol of his non-violence movement. His aim was to introduce spinning and weaving into every home in India, thus providing, on the one hand, home-industry for the poor and, on the other hand, freeing India from dependence on foreign cloth. Every Congressman was pledged to spin and weave so much cloth daily. The national flag was emblazoned with the spinning wheel as the emblem of the movement and *khaddar* (homespun cloth) and Gandhi caps constituted the Congress uniform. *"Spin for Swaraj"* was the slogan of the movement. Gandhi had unbounded faith in the "wheel," as he called it. "If millions spun for *Swaraj,*" he said, "in the spirit of non-violence, there would be no necessity for civil disobedience. It would be a constructive force such as the world has not witnessed before."

Preaching this doctrine with all the fervor of a prophet of old, Gandhi stood forth as the champion of non-violence. Revered as saint and *Mahatma* by millions of his people, he summoned them, not by the sword but by the power of *satyagraha* to a mighty struggle for freedom. This appeal to spiritual force found instant response in the Eastern mind and his followers rose to his call as one man. Non-co-operation swept like a tidal wave over the country. *Ryots* refused to pay taxes. Village officers resigned their posts. Students withdrew from government schools and colleges. The jails were filled with volunteers offering themselves for arrest. High caste women came out from the seclusion of the *zenana,* threw aside the veil, and joined the picket lines. Gandhi volunteers offered *satyagraha* in the public streets and were beaten to pulp by the police, without uttering a murmer. Elsewhere I have told the story of Gandhi's Non-co-operation movement in 1921-22, in which the government was well-nigh paralyzed and brought to the verge of defeat in the darkest days since the Mutiny. This frail little man in a loin cloth, with no weapon in his hand save his own indomitable soul, took on the British Empire and fought it to a standstill. As Pandita Ramabai says: "The straw became a thunder-bolt."

With a stroke of genius, Gandhi dramatized this great struggle in a vivid act. In 1930 he carried out his famous "March to the Sea." Salt in India is a government monopoly and to make or gather it is illegal. Gandhi, therefore, took salt as a symbol. Gathering a band of volunteers he started out from Ahmedabad on his pilgrimage of freedom. Slowly he moved along the hot and dusty road, day by day, as the whole world looked on at the strange sight. In that little band of uncouth men and women crying, *"Gandhi-ki-jai"* was pictured and dramatized India in her ceaseless struggle for freedom. "We asked for bread and they gave us a stone," was the bitter cry of the little band. At last they came to the sea. With his faithful followers gathered about him, Gandhi reached down and scooped up from the water a handful of illicit salt, in open defiance of the British *Raj!* That day a fire was kindled in the hearts of India's sons and daughters that has never been put out!

Gandhi's Philosophy of Suffering

Such a struggle as this, carried on by an unarmed and undisciplined people against the might of a great empire, could not fail to call for suffering and self-sacrifice on the part of the participants. In his autobiography Gandhi gives us his philosophy of suffering as follows:

> Suffering is the mark of the human tribe. It is an eternal law. The mother suffers so that her child may live. Life comes out of death. The condition of wheat growing is that the seed-grain should perish. No country has ever risen without being purified through the fire of suffering . . . . It is impossible to do away with the law of suffering which is the one indispensible condition of our being. Progress is to be measured by the amount of suffering undergone . . . the purer the suffering the greater is the progress.

Mahatma Gandhi's famous fasts have all been based on this principle. Before undertaking his last fast in 1943 he said: "Fasting has a definite place in the scheme of *satyagraha.* It is the last weapon in the armory of non-violence. It is taken by way of penance, purification and protest. I have never made fasting a fad. I have never looked forward to it, although it has often brought solace to the agonized soul, for real fasting puts the soul in tune with its Maker. It puts life into one's prayers. I am praying for light and guidance, without which there will be no fast." Gandhi's first great fast was in 1921, when he fasted in penance for the mob-violence in the awful tragedy of Chauri-Chaura, for which he felt himself in some way responsible. Again in 1923, after a violent outbreak between the Hindus and the Moslems, he fasted twenty-one days to bring the warring parties together in reconciliation. Again in 1932, after his return from the Round Table Conference in London, he underwent a fast "unto death" for the untouchables, in which he sought to secure their rights under the new Constitution. His last great fast was in 1943, which is of special note.

The Poona Fast

After six months' interment in the palace of the Aga Khan at Poona, on February 9, 1943, Gandhi began a three weeks' fast. His purpose, as stated in his letter to the viceroy, was "to appeal to the highest tribunal of justice." The viceroy offered to release him for the duration of the fast, but Gandhi refused. He would not compromise. He would be a symbol of India's struggle for freedom. About the bedside of this frail little man on a bamboo cot in the Aga Khan's palace the whole world gathered in hushed expectancy. Would he survive or would he perish in the attempt? Day by day he grew weaker and weaker. On the twelfth day the crisis came. He could not speak or lift a hand. He seemed to be dying. The doctors said he could not survive unless the fast were broken. Appeals poured in from all over India and even from China and Australia. The Nationalist leader, Sir Tej Badahur Sapru, and two hundred prominent Indian leaders appealed to Prime Minister Winston Churchill to release Gandhi unconditionally, warning that "if Gandhi dies, the task of reconciling the British and the Hindus will be extremely difficult." On report of our Ambassador William Phillips, in India, official circles in Washington were deeply concerned and Secretary Hull conferred with Lord Halifax over the grave situation. In London, the *News Chronicle* in an editorial appealing to Churchill, said:

"Gandhi is dying in captivity. If Gandhi dies, India will never forgive us."

It was a fateful hour. What would the mighty British *Raj* do with this frail little man moving on to death? Here was the opportunity to break the deadlock, to win India by an act of great magnanimity, of wise statesmanship and of high moral courage. Such an act, at such a time, would have electrified India and brought peace and reconciliation to a distraught and despairing people. But Churchill said, "NO." He would not take the risk. He saw only the danger. The larger issues of a free India, bound to Britain by the ties of mutual esteem and good will, he failed to grasp. It was a momentous decision.

Then a miracle happened. After all human powers failed, shall we say, *God intervened.* Gandhi rallied. He began to speak. "God has heard my prayer and the prayer of my people," he cried. The fast was over. But the iron gates of the Aga Khan's palace closed on the frail little man by order of the viceroy and gloom once more settled over India.

The news that Gandhi had ended his fast and survived the ordeal was received with prayers of thanksgiving by millions of his followers and, in fact, by the whole civilized world. But as the iron gates of the palace closed upon him, one could not but ask what had been accomplished by the fast. That things looked pretty dark for the little man could not be denied. After a fast of twenty-one days, in which he had well-nigh perished, Gandhi had not wrung a single concession from the British Raj. His weapon of *satyagraha,* so often infallible in the past, had failed to open the doors of the prison house. On the faces of the little band of faithful followers who gathered about the bedside of the weakened and exhausted little man were plainly written the marks of dismay and consternation. His life-long friend, Rajagopalachari, with profound sadness said, "The British have scored against us." True, the British had "scored." They had closed the iron gates on the little man. But it was the triumph of *force. They* were not the victors. *The frail and emaciated little man lying on the bamboo cot was the victor!* Before the whole world he had made his mighty protest—his appeal to high heaven! Into the very jaws of death he had entered in behalf of freedom which he deemed more precious than life itself! Though shut behind iron bars, he was not conquered. India was not conquered. She would yet be free. *"Gandhi-ki-jai" was still ringing in the air!*

Gandhi's Trial and Imprisonment

Not only did Gandhi undertake great fasts, some of them in penance and others in protest against grave wrongs as he conceived them, but again and again he was cast into prison. In fact all of his fasts, except the first, were undertaken within prison walls. Following his Civil Disobedience movement in 1922, on March 10 he was arrested at Ahmedabad. His trial on that occasion was one of the most remarkable trials recorded in history. It was conducted with the utmost dignity and courtesy and with the utmost consideration for the character of the accused. Gandhi pleaded guilty. Very boldly he addressed the judge as follows:

"I am here to invite and submit cheerfully to the highest penalty that can be inflicted upon me for what, in law, is a deliberate crime, but what appears to me to be the highest duty of a citizen. The only course open to you, the Judge and the assessors, is either to resign your posts and thus dissociate yourselves from evil, or to inflict on me the severest penalty."

The Judge, in passing sentence, said to the prisoner:

"It would be impossible to ignore the fact that in the eyes of millions of your countrymen you are a great patriot and a great leader. But I have to deal with you in one character only. It is my duty to judge you as a man subject to the law, who has, by his own admission, broken the law and committed what to an ordinary man must appear to be a grave offence against such law."

Accordingly, the judge sentenced the *Mahatma* to six years' imprisonment. On receiving the sentence, Gandhi smilingly thanked the judge. So ended one of the most remarkable trials in history.

Gandhi and the Cross

It is not too much to say that the trial and imprisonment of Mahatma Gandhi turned the thoughts of India leaders in a remarkable way to the trial and death of Christ. In his address to the Indian National Congress in 1923, Mr. C. R. Dass, the president, referring to the trial and imprisonment of Mahatma Gandhi, quoted at length the last chapters of the Gospel of Matthew, describing the trial and crucifixion of Christ. So far had the mind of India moved, linking their great leader with Christ in the supreme tragedy of history! A distinguished Hindu declared: "Mahatma Gandhi has, by his trial, done something which the missionary has not been able to do in fifty years, namely he has turned the eyes of India to the Cross." This is a remarkable testimony from a Hindu and it is true. By his life of privation and self-sacrifice, by his oft-repeated fastings in great crises in the national life, by his trial and imprisonment for the cause to which he had devoted his life, Mahatma Gandhi turned the mind of India towards Christ. India never knew the meaning of the Cross before. Now she has seen Gandhi and she knows. In him, one of her own sons, she has caught the vision of the Cross. Gandhi by his suffering has made the Cross intelligible to the Hindu mind. She has seen in him the power of vicarious suffering. In some mysterious way, moved by the sacrificial life and sufferings of her great leader, India has been drawn to the Christ of Calvary.

When Gandhi finished his great fast for freedom within the prison walls of the Aga Khan's palace at Poona, gathered about the bedside of the weakened and exhausted leader the little band of devoted followers sang a hymn—not a hymn from the sacred books of the Hindus, but a CHRISTIAN hymn! Gandhi called for his favorite hymn and this they sang:

> **When I survey the wondrous Cross**
> **On which the Prince of Glory died,**
> **My richest gain I count but loss**
> **And pour contempt on all my pride.**

Victory in Death

On January 30, 1948, as he was going to his evening prayer meeting in Birla's garden, New Delhi, Mahatma Gandi was assassinated by a Hindu fanatic. The whole world mourns the passing of a great soul and servant of humanity—martyr to the cause he loved and for which he gave his life.

In the providence of God, Mahatma Gandhi lived to see fulfilled his dream of a free and independent India. However dark the hour, however long and arduous the way, he never doubted India would be free. Even after the attainment of that great goal, Mahatma Gandhi had visions of guiding India through the difficult days of transition, which he well knew were sure to come, ere India could take her place among the great nations of the earth.

But it was not to be. Like a flash of lightning, in a moment, the assassin's shot rang out in Birla's garden, and the great soul fell, mortally wounded, into the arms of his attendants. The nation stood aghast, stunned by the awful blow!

But the hand of God was in it. His work was done. His hour had come. God called him home. In death Mahatma Gandhi is greater than in life. He is not dead. He lives. His work goes on. He lives in the hearts and lives of all who have felt the quickening touch of his spirit and all who have heard his brave, clear call to peace and goodwill, be he Hindu, Moslem or Sikh, white or black. He has joined the ranks of the Immortals.

XVI

THE SILENT REVOLUTION: MOVEMENTS OF THE SPIRIT

In one of his famous meetings for the intellectuals of India Dr. Stanley Jones was speaking of the slow progress of Christianity in India. At the close of the meeting a *Brahman* gentleman came up to him and said: "Sir, you need not be discouraged. You do not know how far your Gospel has gone."

No one knows how far the Gospel has gone in India—in how many hearts it has found lodgment, into how many homes it has entered, what winds are wafting it along, what "tides of the Spirit" are bearing it on, what forces deep down in the hearts of the people are sweeping it to its final consumation. In many ways, unseen and unknown, mysterious as the blowing of the wind, the Kingdom of God comes. We cannot gauge its coming by statistics nor measure its progress by baptisms. When I tell you there are nine million Christians in India among four hundred million people, you may well say, "What are these among so many." But these figures do not tell the story. The Kingdom cometh not with observation. We cannot say, "Lo, here! Lo, there!" The Kingdom is "within." It is "spirit and life." Silently and irresistably, like the rising of the ocean tides, it comes. As the Spirit of God moved of old in creative power on the face of the waters, so the Spirit is moving today in the unrest, the turmoil, the strife, in this ancient land, bringing to birth in the hearts of the people new ideals, new hopes and new aspirations. Great movements, political, social and religious, are sweeping over the land, breaking down barriers, revolutionizing thought and life and preparing the hearts of the people for the coming of the Kingdom.

Breaking Down the Walls of Caste

One of the most momentous and revolutionary movements going on in India today is the disintegration of caste. Undoubtedly the greatest obstacle to the spread of Christianity in India is the caste system. Originally there were only four castes—the *Brahman* or Priest, the *Kshatryya* or Warrior, the *Vasyya* or Merchant and the *Sudra* or Farmer. Today each caste is split up into hundreds of sub-castes. Among the Brahmans alone there are said to be some two hundred sects. And beneath all these castes and beyond the pale of Hinduism, are the outcastes— the untouchables. Under this caste system a man's status in society is fixed by birth. As he is born so must he be. If he is born a pariah he must be a pariah forever. Dr. Ramji Ambedkar, principal of the law college, Bombay, is a distinguished scholar, holding degrees from the University of London, Bonn and Columbia; but he was born an outcaste and he cannot escape the stigma of his birth. Hindu society is divided into water-tight compartments, fixed, rigid and immovable. Man is separated from man by insuperable barriers which he can never surmount and never break down. Interdining and intermarriage are absolutely prohibited. Even the shadow of the outcaste must not fall on the Brahman and his touch is pollution. To become a Christian is to break with Hindu society—to become an outcaste, to be driven from home, from father and mother and wife and child, to lose all and henceforth to be dead to one's people. This is what it means for a high caste Hindu to become a Christian. Caste is the well-nigh insurmountable barrier to the progress of Christianity among the higher classes in India.

However, under the impact of Western civilization and the silent and ceaseless working of the Spirit of God, this mighty rock of Hinduism which has stood unshaken for forty centuries, is beginning to crumble. When we first went to India some fifty years ago, our Brahman friends often came to visit us in our home, bringing garlands of flowers and the inevitable betel-nut and lime. With evident reluctance and the lightest possible touch, they would shake hands, but when they went home they would not fail to take a bath; and as for taking a cup of tea, that was an abomination. Today the tea party is the favorite social diversion of the educated Indian. Whenever one of our officials is leaving the station, there is a round of dinner and tea parties in his honor at which *Brahmans, Sudras,* Mohammedans, Europeans, Christians and pariahs sit down at a common board and eat together.

When the municipal water works were introduced into Kurnool some forty years ago, some orthodox *Brahmans* at first refused to use the water and continued to go to the Tungabadhra River a full half mile away, but very soon all classes were drawing water from a common faucet. The railroad trains in India with accomodation for first, second and third class passengers are crowded with natives. But only officials and wealthy Indians travel first and second class. Rather than pay double and treble fare the *Brahman* and high caste man often pockets his pride and his scruples, purchases a third class ticket and is shoved unceremoniously by the guard into a third class compartment, occupied by twelve or fifteen passangers of promiscuous castes or no caste at all. The Iron Horse in its march across the continent of India has not only levelled hills and mountains; it is a mighty leveller of Hindu society as well. In the olden days to go to England and cross the "black water," as the Hindus say, meant sure excommunication, and it was only after

The "Iron Horse" comes to Kurnool, 1905. Celebrating the opening of the railway to Kurnool. Mrs. Stanton and the three children are on the right.

paying the heaviest penalties that one could be re-instated into caste. Today the British steamers are crowded with scores and hundreds of high caste Hindus—students going to Oxford and Cambridge to complete their education; honorable members of the Indian Legislature, commissioned on high political affairs before the British Parliament, commercial men, exploiting the famous products of the Far East; Indian princes, maharajas, and maharanis, travelling with their gaudy retinues, bent on visiting the famous resorts of European capitals, and even high caste *Brahman* women, just emerging from the age-long seclusion of the *Zenanà*.

In our mission schools and colleges the *Brahman,* the *Sudra,* the Mohammedan, the Christian and the pariah sit side by side, read the same books, study the same lessons, and compete for prizes in scholarship in which often the outcaste lad comes out the victor. On the football and hockey field they rub shoulder to shoulder in many a hard-fought contest. In all the varied activities of school life these boys are learning the great lessons of fraternity and brotherhood. Caste can scarcely survive the free air of the classroom and the comradeship of the football game. Here barriers are broken down, caste distinctions fade away and life-friendships are formed. Today a very large number of educated Hindus have definitely renounced caste and boldly take their stand against it both in public and private. The late Sir Rabindranath Tagore belonged to one of the most famous *Brahman* families of Bengal, but no one ever thought of Tagore as a *Brahman.* He was the inspired poet, the voice of the East, the prophet of the New Day! In 1936 the Maharaja of Travancore, one of the most enlightened, but at the same time one of the most orthodox of Hindus, by an edict on his twenty-fourth birthday, threw open the ancient, sacred temples of his state to the untouchables—an act which stirred all India to its foundations.

In this ancient land there are many sad sights, many grave wrongs. Age-long evils, deeply rooted in the social and religious life of the people cry out for redress. The wrongs of Indian womanhood—who can depict them! The wrongs of the little child-wife, married at six and a mother at twelve. How often have I seen her standing at the door of her house, holding her tiny baby in her tiny arms! No wonder that one third of the babies in India die before they are a year old! The wrongs of the little child-widow, shorn of her beautiful hair, stripped of her jewels, clad in the coarse garments of perpetual widowhood, with the curses of gods and men resting on her inocent head; the blighting seclusion of the *zenana* with its doors and windows bolted and barred by the frail hands of Indian women; the ignorance and superstition of the women of well-nigh all classes, only two per cent of whom can read and write; the corrupting influence of the dancing girls in the *Nautch;* the sad fate of the *Devadasis* or temple girls, married to the god in infancy and dedicated in the name of religion to a life of open shame—all these deep seated wrongs of Hindu society are at last beginning to come home to the mind and conscience of educated India and to cry out for redress.

Homes are being opened for widows and a determined effort made to ameliorate the sad condition of these unfortunate ones. Women are coming out of the seclusion of the *zenana* and beginning to take their rightful place in the life of the nation. Widow remarriage, though not frequent, is steadily increasing. A few years ago in Madras the marriage of a high caste *Brahman* with a pariah girl, an outcaste, was celebrated with great eclat. In the Sarda Act of 1929, passed by the Central Legislative Assembly at New Delhi, the marriagable age of girls was raised to fourteen and that of boys to eighteen, the Bill being passed entirely by the votes of Hindus and Mohammedans. *Fifty* years ago when we went to Kurnool no marriage could be celebrated and no social function held without the entertainment of the *Nautch.* Today the *Nautch* has been banished in respectable society and enlightened men will not attend a party where it is introduced. Very strong agitation also has developed for the abolition of the *Devadasis* and the liberation of these unfortunate ones from a life of shame. Many sincere and earnest souls among the enlightened leaders in India today are boldly pressing for reform along all these lines and in the face of bitter opposition by the orthodox party are steadily and persistently seeking to eradicate from Hindu society these age-old evils. More and more the conscience of India is becoming sensitive to evil.

In the last two decades a great change has come over Indian womanhood. Gandhi's call to Indian women to participate in his Non-co-operation movement was responded to by hundreds and thousands of women in all ranks of life, many of whom went to jail in defense of the cause they had espoused. Under the Act of 1935 of the new Constitution, six million women were enfranchised and forty-two seats in the provincial and central legislatures were reserved for them. Eight women have attained Cabinet rank in the provincial governments as deputy speakers and parliamentary secretaries. Mrs. Vijayalakshmi Pandit, sister of Jawaharlal Nehru, proved herself a very able Minister of Health in the government of her province and is now Ambassador to U.S.A. Three Indian women had the honor to be sent as delegates to the Round Table Conference in London—Mrs. Sarojini Naidu, Nationalist leader, orator and poet (one of the most gifted women of our time); Begum Shah Nawaz, the most prominent Moslem woman in public life; and Mrs. Subbarayam, one of the most cultured women in Madras.

The All-India Women's Conference, meeting in convention each year, is a most remarkable gathering of the educated and enlightened women of New India, supporting in its resolutions every progressive movement in India and often taking the lead on questions of social and religious reform. Today, in this ancient land, we are witnessing the birth of a new Indian womanhood.

The New Spirit of Swadeshism

There is no doubt that a new spirit has come over India—a spirit of self-consciousness and self-help. The old spirit of servility and dependence is gone or fast disappearing. Things Indian are at a premium and things Western at a discount. *Swadeshi* goods, *Swadeshi* stores, *Swadeshi* mills, *Swadeshi* banks and even *Swadeshi* schools are the rage of the day. India for the Indians is the cry. The extremists would even drive the Englishman out of the country and the moderate hardly knows whether he wants him or not. After the long sleep of centuries India is beginning to feel the stirring of a new life and is ambitious to take her place among the free nations of the earth. This unrest, while primarily political, affects in no small degree the work of missions. The missionary comes in for his share of the general dislikes of the foreigner. In many parts of Bengal and even in Calcutta mission schools have had to be closed, Sunday schools disbanded and bazaar preaching discontinued. A few years ago in Madras popular feeling was so aroused over the conversion of a Hindu girl that every Hindu home was closed to missionary ladies for months and it was impossible to carry on *zenana* work in the city or even to hold religious services in preaching halls. Even where such opposition is not manifested, undoubtedly the educated classes do not look to the missionary as in the past. We must acknowledge that at present the drift in many quarters is away from us. The people are impatient of foreign guidance and want a free hand to work out their future. So-called "national" schools are springing up on every side and the mission school no longer holds its supremacy. Hindu young men's associations, street preaching bands and even missions to the outcastes are being organized and actively propagated. We recognize that much of this is spasmodic and done simply to show what India can do. So we do not need to be greatly disturbed by it. The opportunity is still great.

This movement, however, is not without its hopeful aspect. This very spirit of Swadeshism is what we have long been trying to develop in the Indian church. To get her to stand on her feet, to bear her burdens and to cut loose from mission leading-strings has been the great problem in the past. If, then, this new spirit of self-help once takes hold of the Indian church, we may expect great things in the future. If among all the *Swadeshi* enterprises in India, the Indian church also becomes *Swadeshi,* then indeed will we witness the dawn of a new day for Christianity in this land. When the Indian church really comes to her own, as India is coming to her own, and feels the stirring of the new life within her, when she awakes to the consciousness of her great mission in this land—then may we expect her to be girded with a new power and to go forth to victory. The problem then is one of re-adjustment, to carry over the spirit of self-help into the Indian church and to utilize these new forces for the Kingdom of God.

The Revival of Hinduism

Swadeshism cries aloud in the streets and is raising a great hubbub in the land. It is easy to think, therefore, that this is all there is of it, as doubtless it is with many. But the most significant movement in India today is not political but religious. Along with the aspiration for self-government and political independence and, indeed, much deeper than that, is the aspiration for a satisfying faith. India is today in quest of a religion. Too proud to accept the religion of her rulers and too aroused intellectually to longer cling to the gross polytheism of the masses, she is searching her sacred books anew and seeking to find in her *Vedas* and *Upanishads* a soul-satisfying religion. Now for more than a century the fierce white light of Christianity has been beating on this ancient system, revealing its weaknesses, its superstitions and its corruptions. At first, it seemed as if Hinduism must inevitably fall before the onslaught. In the early days of the nineteenth century, in the days of Alexander Duff in Calcutta, John Wilson in Bombay and John Anderson in Madras, some of the greatest minds in India became captive to Christ. Keshub Chandar Sen, founder of the *Brahmo Samaj,* thundered out before the world: *"Christ, none but Christ, shall have the fair diadem of India!"* But the battle was not so easily won. Hinduism gathered herself for a last great struggle. She was ready to abandon all else. *Puranas, tanthras,* traditions, laws, customs—all might go, if only the heart of the ancient faith, the essence of the Hindu religion—the *Vedanta,* were retained. Behind the *Vedanta* philosophy, "the summit of human reason," as she holds, she entrenched herself. Her sacred Scriptures were the *Vedas* and the *Upanishads.* Her Gospel was the *Bhagavadgita* (the Divine Song). Giving up all else, on this rock she would build her house. The latter half of the nineteenth century was the Reformation period in the history of the Hindu religion. From that period it emerged as a new, powerful and aggressive force in the life of the nation.

It is the old story of the struggle of the ancient religions and philosophies of Greece and Rome against the triumphant advance of Christianity. History repeats itself. The old battle is being fought again on the plains of India. Mother of religions, she is to contend at last with a religion that has made its triumphant way over half the globe. What, then, is the situation today? We find a tremendous change along the whole front. When we condemn Polytheism and point to India's three hundred and thirty-three million gods, she says, "There is but one God. All these are but names—manifestations of *Paramatma*—the Supreme Spirit, the Ultimate Reality." When we rebuke her for the worship of idols, she says, "These are for the common herd who are incapable of spiritual worship and must needs have some outward form before their eyes. We worship God as a Spirit." When we tell her that she has no Christ, she points to the *Rama* of the *Mahabarata* and the *Krishna* of the *Bhagavadgita*. When we tell her that God is personal, she takes direct issue with us and says: "Brahma, the *Atman* (Spirit) is Impersonal, *Nirguna* (without attributes) and "beyond the reach of thought and voice."

And so the field is cleared. The issues are drawn. Christianity is face to face with her fiercest foe. Hinduism today is putting forth her best, her highest. Like the blind Samson of old, she is gathering herself for the last supreme struggle. Thank God for this. The issue is not doubtful. Only thus can the final victory be won. Only when Hinduism has put forth her highest and best and come to see, deep down in her inmost soul, that she is but feeding on ashes will she turn at last in helplessness from the *Bhagavadgita* to the Gospel of the Son of God!

The struggle is on. The work of missions the past century in India has been largely a work of reconnoitering and skirmishing, with here and there the taking of a few outposts. But we are coming to close quarters now and the death-struggle with Hinduism has begun. In this mighty conflict we must use the choicest weapons of Christianity. We must seize upon the central and fundamental truths of our religion, relegating all else to the background, and press them home with irresistable power upon the hearts and consciences of the people. We must make our message perfectly clear so that there can be no confusing of issues or misunderstanding of what Christianity is. And above all, we must persistently hold forth *Christ as the Desire of all nations, the Fulfiller of all Prophesy and all Oracles of all time, the Light that lighteth every man that cometh into the world.*

The Movement toward Christ

In the midst of this mighty struggle, this supreme effort of Hinduism to save its life, as it were, another movement is sweeping over India. It is a movement of the mind of India toward Christ. In some mysterious way, unknown and inexplicable, India has caught the vision of the Christ—not the Christ of the West, but the Christ of the East, the Christ of the Gallilean Lake, the Christ of Olivet, the Christ of the Garden and the Cross. A Brahman said to Stanley Jones: "I don't like the Christ of your creeds and churches." Then said Stanley Jones, "How would you like the Christ of the Indian Road?" The man was silent for a moment, picturing to himself the Christ by the wayside, healing the sick, ministering to the suffering, cleansing the leper, bearing the Cross up Calvary's steps. Then quietly he said, "I could love and follow the Christ of the Indian Road." That Christ has seized the imagination of the best minds in India today. At the Indian National Congress at Poona thirty years ago, when the name of Christ was mentioned, it was greeted with a very hostile demonstration. Ten years later, in his address to the Indian National Congress, the President, referring to the trial and imprisonment of Gandhi, their great leader, quoted at length from the last chapters of the Gospel of Matthew, describing the trial and crucifixion of Christ. The reading produced a profound impression.

Dr. Charles W. Gilkey was the Barrows Lecturer in India in 1925. Very boldly, but astutely, he chose as the subject of his lectures "The Personality of Jesus." He delivered the series of lectures in all the leading cities of India. The largest halls were not able to accomodate the crowds of educated Hindus and Mohammedans who flocked to hear him on this high theme. President MacMichen of the Wilson College, Bombay, said to Dr. Gilkey, "If you had chosen that subject five years ago or even three, you would have had no bearing. I am amazed at this burst of interest and these crowds." Mr. K. Naturajan, Editor of the *Indian Social Reformer* and one of the leading social thinkers in India, remarked in his paper; "The Barrows lecturer could not have chosen a subject of more vital interest in India today than the subject of "The Personality of Jesus." In their tour of India Dr. and Mrs. Gilkey came to Kurnool and we had the honor of entertaining them in our home. A public meeting was held in our beautiful Coles Centennial Church which seats twelve hundred people. The church was packed to the doors with a great audience of the leading Hindu and Mohammedan gentlemen of the town. Speaking for more than an hour, Dr. Gilkey delivered a powerful and moving address on Christ which gripped and held the audience spellbound.

The remarkable work which Dr. Stanley Jones has been carrying on among the educated classes in India for many years is well known to all. In his famous books, *The Christ of the Indian Road* and *Christ at the Round Table,* he has told the fascinating story. Travelling from one end of India to the other, he has preached Christ and Christ only. Everywhere great throngs of the intellectuals of India have waited on his word. Some thirty years ago when John R. Mott spoke in Madras and mentioned the name of Christ, the Hindus hissed. Five years later Stanley Jones spoke in Madras for six nights on "Jesus and Him Crucified" and the hall was packed to the doors, night after night. The last night, on invitation, one hundred and fifty young men came forward and took their stand for Christ. When Stanley Jones was in Tinnevilly, Bishop Tubbs of the Church of England remarked:

> "I had no idea of the vast change that has come over the mind of India in these twenty years. I remember that twenty years ago Sherwood Eddy talked for fifty-five minutes to an audience of Hindus and Mohammedans at Allabad before they would allow him to speak the last five minutes on Christ. It was a very hostile audience that he faced. But here you begin at once on Christ, have no other theme and the best men in the city are asking for more. There is a vast psychological and spiritual change."[1]

At his meetings Stanley Jones has a Hindu or a Mohammedan gentleman preside as chairman and at the close he throws the meeting open for questions. This question hour, when the keenest minds in India fire questions at him, is a grueling time, and no one but a man like Stanley Jones could stand up to it. In the course of these discussions many remarkable testimonies are given. Said a Hindu: "If you preach this kind of a Christ to us, just Christ Himself, then we Hindus will all worship Him."[2]

Another said: "There was a time when none of us in India wanted to claim Christ, but now everybody is trying to claim Him."[3]

Another said: "We have been talking to the dumb silences, and Jesus is the voice that has answered us."[4]

A Hindu chairman of one of the meetings said: "There are none of us now among thoughtful Hindus who have not a reverence for Christ."[5]

[1] E. Stanley Jones, **Christ at the Round Table**, p. 320-21. Abingdon Press. [2] Ibid, p. 319. [3] Ibid, p. 322. [4] Ibid, p. 276. [5] Ibid, p. 150.

This marvellous change which is coming over the mind of India in its attitude toward Christ is vividly set forth in the following incident related by Stanley Jones. He asked one of the out-standing philosophers of India—a man deeply versed in the philosophy both of the East and the West. "What do you think of Jesus Christ?" After a minute's silence, the man replied:

"We had high ideas of God before Jesus came. But Jesus is the highest expression of God we have seen. He is conquering us by the sheer force of His personality, even against our will" *

In this hour of awakening, India turns toward Christ. She has worshipped at a thousand shrines. She has built her temples on every high hill and under every wide-spreading tree. She has sought salvation in the solitude of the forest and in the caves and dens of the mountains. She has toiled along the dusty pilgrim roads in pain and anguish. She has bathed in the sacred waters of the Ganges. She has crucified herself on beds of spikes and given her body to be burned. She has renounced the world and the fashion thereof, which she calls *Maya* (illusion) that she might win *Mukti* (release) from the endless cycle of births and re-births, falling at last into the Infinite bosom of *Brahma!*

The long night of India's toil is far spent. The day dawns. The Sun of Righteousness is rising over the plains of India with healing in his beams. The heavens are opened and there comes a voice saying: "This is my Beloved Son, hear ye Him." And the Son cries with a voice to wake the dead: "If any man thirst, let him come unto Me and drink." It is the voice of the Good Shepherd, calling His sheep. It is the voice of the Bridegroom, saying, "Come." It is the voice of the Saviour, calling the weary and heavy-laden: "Come unto

* E. Stanley Jones, **The Christ of the Indian Road,** p. 216-17. Abingdon Press.

Me and I will give you rest."

India has heard that voice in these last days and it has stirred her deepest soul. Many voices of priest and prophet have spoken to her through the long ages of the past, but no voice so sweet, so tender, so low, has ever before sounded in her ears. And as she listens and longs and lingers, she says: "Truly it is the voice of God—the 'accent of the Holy Ghost.' "

It was Christmas Eve in the *Ashram* of the famous Bangali poet, Sir Rabindranath Tagore, at Shantiniketan, the "Abode of Peace." The little company of his friends and followers had gathered there at the invitation of the poet, not to chant the praises of Hindu gods, but to commemorate the birth of Christ! And as they gathered in the eventide, the poet gave his message in these words:

"Let us bow to Jesus Christ who revealed to man the Divinity of Love."

How strange a scene!

A Christian service in a Hindu Ashram in memory of Christ—the Revealer of Divine Love!

How strange and yet how fitting! Wise Men of the East, as of old, worshipping at the feet of Christ! Shall not India do likewise?

Land of the shimmering sea and stately palm,
Recurrent restlessness, majestic calm;
Land of the sun-parched plain and snow-pearled peak,
Sublimely strong, pathetically weak!
Land of Unfathomed age, yet fount of youth,
Swiftest yet slowest in the Quest for Truth!

Of old, in cell and cave and hermitage,
In forest dim, dwelt many a saintly sage,
Striving by prayer and penance for the key
To ope the door of Karma and be free;
Yet millions now bow down to wood and stone
That haply they may find the Great Unknown!

"Land of the Quest, I hear within thy breast
The throb of that great heart that yearns for rest.
I come to claim thee," thus Master saith,
"I am the goal of all thy groping faith,
Thy longing and thy love. Come unto Me.
Thy Quest is ended. I will make thee free!"